m
media
MANUAL

Basic TV Reporting

media
MANUAL

Basic
TV Reporting

2nd Edition

Ivor Yorke

Focal Press
An imprint of Butterworth-Heinemann
Linacre House, Jordan Hill, Oxford OX2 8DP
A division of Reed Educational and Professional Publishing Ltd

℞ A member of the Reed Elsevier plc group

OXFORD   BOSTON   JOHANNESBURG
MELBOURNE   NEW DELHI   SINGAPORE

First published 1990
Reprinted 1994, 1995
Second edition 1997

British Library Cataloguing in Publication Data
A catalogue record for this book is available from the British Library

Library of Congress Cataloguing in Publication Data
A catalogue record for this book is available from the Library of Congress

ISBN 0 240 51434 3

Typeset by David Gregson Associates, Beccles, Suffolk
Printed and bound in Great Britain

Contents

Acknowledgements from First Edition

I am particularly grateful to all those who have provided illustrations or helped with picture research in the preparation of this book.

Special thanks therefore to James Feltham and Graham Milloy of BBC Central Stills; Anthony Painter, Picture Editor, Sky; Chris Lambert, Broadcast Developments Ltd, Autoscript; Autocue; Brian Barker, EDS Portaprompt; Hans Rietveld, Key West, Holland; Quantel; Tim Orchard, for trusting me with souvenirs from his US assignments; the International Press Institute for permission to quote from *Journalists on Dangerous Assignments*; Colin Shaw, Director of the Broadcasting Standards Council, for permission to reproduce parts of their draft code; Phil Ashworth and Sarah Finley for acting as models for some of the illustrations.

Thanks too, to those who kindly read through all or part of the manuscript and offered me the benefit of their professional advice: Bernard Hesketh, Mike Scarlett, Tom Wragg, and finally Rob Kirk, Editor of Thames News, who reminded me that while reporting is a serious, responsible and (according to some) a glamorous business, it's also more often than not, a lot of *fun*.

Ivor Yorke

Ivor Yorke was a journalist on local newspapers and in Fleet Street before joining BBC Television News as a sub-editor in 1964. He went on to become a reporter, producer and editor on a wide range of BBC news programmes. After six years as Head of Journalist Training, he left the BBC in 1992 to establish his own training consultancy.

Sadly, Ivor died before he had time to complete this new edition of his book and we are indebted to Ray Alexander – the current manager and Senior Instructor, Television at BBC News Training – for finalising the task and so allowing the book to remain in print as a memorial to Ivor's significant contribution to the field of broadcast journalism training.

Introduction

Of all the journalists and technicians involved in the production of television news and news-related programmes throughout the world, it is safe to say few if any arouse more interest, envy and controversy than the 'Talent' – those whose good fortune it is to appear before the public as on-screen presenters or reporters. Ask almost any aspiring young broadcast journalist for the 'ideal' career, and ten to one he or she will reel off an impressive list of names of those whose exploits they have followed keenly through their reporting from the world's trouble-spots, and whom they would dearly love to emulate given the opportunity. For no matter how strongly it is argued that power and responsibility reside largely with desk-bound producers and editors, it is difficult to persuade the young not to be dazzled by the glamour of appearing on television in front of millions. The urge to share the same 'front seat on history' international television reporters take as a normal part of their everyday working lives continues to draw the young and ambitious like a powerful drug.

None but the faint-hearted will be deterred by the increased physical risks involved in some areas of modern-day reporting – that, sadly, has become news in its own right – but what most will not be in a position to appreciate is how broadcast journalism has been undergoing a revolution which makes 'reporting' for television a vastly more complex occupation than before. New technology has made 'multi-skilling' an economic proposition for a growing number of news organisations, with journalists encouraged to reach modest standards of competence in picture editing and, more controversially, perhaps, operation of the camera on location. 'Bi-media' working, requiring the ability to apply television and radio skills, has its own obvious attractions for employers operating in both spheres. Taken with a changed broadcasting environment in which permanent staff jobs are at a premium, the journalist asking the questions is as likely to have a technical background as an editorial one, the term 'reporter' – in its currently recognised form – may well need to be redefined before long.

Until that happens most young aspirants will at least acknowledge that the road to their desired goal is likely to be a difficult one, although few may stop to consider whether they are physically or mentally equipped for the role. All the rest want to know is the price they have to pay for success and how to get to the front of the queue jostling at the foot of the ladder.

The first thing they need to be told is that many of the most successful television reporters have served an apprenticeship behind the scenes or in print or radio journalism before getting their chance to appear in front of the camera. And while some news organisations are prepared to risk taking on reporters who have no experience or training, others insist that potential on-screen talent comes through strictly defined routes which make allowance for careful grooming and instruction along the way.

Not all beginners can expect to have that professional education, or indeed exposure to the better college courses which mix the practicalities with the theory. For those, hundreds of questions remain about style, technique and presentation.

This book aims to give them some of the answers.

What a Reporter Does

Few of those who aspire to careers as television reporters have more than a vague notion of exactly what the job entails. The evidence is there on the screen 24 hours a day – but how reporters function, where their responsibilities begin and end, and how they link into the editorial chain is not so obvious. The public may also be forgiven for confusing the role of the reporter with that of anchor/newscaster or presenter, because the duties sometimes overlap. Reporting may indeed be seen as a natural stepping-stone to the safety and warmth of the studio, but once installed as part of the news-processing as opposed to news-gathering team, reporters are usually less originators of their own material than shapers of other people's.

Origins of television journalism
Once you become a television journalist you join a young profession with its roots chiefly in newspapers, magazines and radio. It can be a confusing world. Many of those who work in it cannot quite bring themselves to admit they are part of show business, but job titles which once reflected a bond with print journalism are disappearing as broadcast journalist, editor, producer, video-journalist and other televisual terms become more established.

Reporting responsibilities
The role you have to fulfil depends entirely on your employer and the agenda of programme for which you are working. Local, regional, national and international newscasts each make their own demands. In some organisations you will be treated separately as a specialist: in others you will be expected to double up as a picture editor or camera operator.

Whatever title or additional duties you may be expected to undertake, your main task will be to 'get the story'. This will invariably mean taking editorial responsibility for the content and shape of an entire item – assessing on the spot the newsworthiness of an event and the people in it, carrying out interviews, performing a piece to camera and recording a voice-over commentary, as well as co-ordinating the activities of support staff. You may also have to attend to the logistics of deadlines. No 'Brownie points' are won for a brilliant piece of work which arrives too late for inclusion in the programme for which it was intended. You may also expect to broadcast 'live'.

But do not imagine you will spend all your working life on the road. You will be newsroom-bound for a large proportion of the time, engaged in tracking down leads, writing scripts or providing the voice-over for incoming agency pictures or compilations.

1. Conducts research on the spot

2. Decides content and shape

3. Supervises camera operator

4. Carries out interviews

5. Does piece to camera

6. Writes and records voice-over

7. Maintains base links

What a reporter does
In the field reporters are in charge of covering stories as the representatives of their programmes or news organisations. Responsibility includes management of the camera crew as well as control of editorial content. In some organisations the reporter will double as camera-operator and/or picture editor.

13

The TV reporter is part of a team.

A Place on the Taxi Rank

Unless yours is a small organisation where reporters are expected to be 'self-starters' providing all their own ideas, your first responsibility as a newcomer will be to that part of the operation dealing with news gathering. Intake/input/the assignments desk/news desk decides which events are worthy of coverage and assigns staff to cover them. The 'desk' controls your reporting life on behalf of the news editor, who is also likely to give you experience of intake work by assigning you to act as a stand-in occasionally.

The predictability of news
News is a far more predictable phenomenon than it may seem, and a large proportion of every news-related programme appears as a result of good intelligence about events before they take place. Advance information on matters both routine and important flows never-endingly into the headquarters of every news organisation from a myriad of official and unofficial sources, to form the basis of a diary from which conventional daily programmes are constructed. The unexpected nature of the rest of the news means that reporters are sometimes matched with stories simply as they arise. Not for nothing is the reporters' room sometimes known as the 'taxi rank'.

Correspondents, in effect more senior reporters, may have more of a roving commission, and so exercise greater influence on the coverage of events not on the diary. Other news-related programmes, whose commitments may be over longer periods, operate very differently. Here the reporter may be part of a team involved in researching items, or may be contracted to provide an acceptable voice and face at the conclusion of a detailed planning process carried out by others.

In the field
If you have worked in newspapers or radio you will probably have operated alone. As a television reporter you are one of a team. Despite the drift in some quarters to the single video-journalist, the likelihood is you will be supported by a separate camera-operator. Sound recordists and lighting assistants are also to be found on some assignments, as are field producers/directors acting as links with the camera crew.

Editing your report
Your responsibility for covering a news item, once completed, usually passes along the editorial chain to a picture editor, who assembles the raw material for broadcast. Sometimes you may be expected to supervise this work: otherwise it is a producer or programme editor who makes the decisions about content and duration, picture and sound. As 'multi-skilling' takes hold more reporters are expected to edit their own material, having been trained how to use the equipment.

The editorial chain
The reporter represents a single link in the editorial chain, which beings with the idea for a story and ends with its transmission as part of a programme. Where news-related programmes split editorial responsibilities, reporters belong to one group of journalists (intake/input/assignments) devoted to gathering the news. The other (output) processes and prepares the material for broadcast.

What Makes a Good Reporter

What makes a good reporter for television is what makes a good journalist in any other medium, only more so.

The forces which drive most who embark on a career in the profession – a 'nose' for news, born scepticism, hunger for truth and knowledge, and the desire to communicate – have to be weighed against qualities of a more physically obvious nature. At the minimum these consist of a reasonable appearance and a voice of acceptable broadcast standard (see page 42). More than that you will need to develop a thick skin, a touch of arrogance, and the determination not to be deterred by the number of other news people who congregate at the scene of important events.

Persistence ... and sensitivity
Do not expect to be able to hide in the crowd and still succeed, because no television organisation involved in the business of topical journalism could live for long with the regular failure of their man or woman visibly to get the story. The nature of the job is inherently high-profile, so it is sometimes necessary to push through the scrum to get the interview. Quotes cannot be invented for the camera.

In contrast, the good television reporter is expected to know intuitively how to react in situations which call for sensitivity and thoughtfulness. There must be tact, sympathy and an ability to recognise when the moment has come to withdraw discreetly from pursuit of a story in which, say, lives have been lost.

A love of language
It is taken for granted that every would-be journalist can write. The ability to spell is thought by some not to be as important. What is not in doubt is that good reporters should have a natural feel for language, an instinct for the right word at the right time. But since most television insists that its precious air time is not wasted, the pressure is on to produce material which is disciplined, spare and economical. The salient points of every item must be marshalled sensibly and coherently, the language stripped to its bare bones and put to work alongside the pictures.

An eye for illustration
Although it is the camera operator's responsibility to gather the pictures, the good reporter develops an understanding of the visual element. The golden rule is that words and pictures must go together. Divergence leads to competition between the two, distracting the audience. In that case, picture-power will always win.

What makes a good reporter

Reporters, either alone or with the crew, must demonstrate both patience and tenacity. Some events are controlled (top) such as the grabbed interviews at a major event. But it is still a tight squeeze as newsgatherers jostle for position. The street scrum (above) as the subject appears and keeps walking makes it a challenge for the news people to try to ensure the best sound and vision. The reporter could have been waiting for hours for this, but when the event happens the battle for the best coverage begins and ends in a few minutes. In this situation a good reporter not only has to get the questions in, but should also watch the camera crew's back.

The Reporter as Manager

As we approach the end of the century, a team working on location for a typical news programme is likely to consist of no more than two people – a reporter and a camera-operator. Until the single 'video-journalist' becomes an industry standard, knowing how to be an effective leader will remain an integral part of the reporter's job. Being in charge of the camera-operator usually goes with editorial responsibility for the story. Strong-willed professionals inevitably have differences of opinion from time to time, making 'management' a daunting prospect, but even as a newcomer you must always be assertive, take the lead and set the pace. At all times know what you want: inexperienced or freelance camera crews will expect to follow your instructions, sometimes to the letter.

Reporter–camera operator relationship
Because every television report should be the result of a combination of creative processes, a positive working relationship between reporter and camera-operator is far more likely to produce successful results than one in which the two are at odds with each other. In some circumstances how far you are united in your determination to pursue a news story could make the difference between life and death.

Trust and interdependability work both ways. Nothing damns a reporter more quickly in the eyes of the camera-operator than arrogance and unreliability, especially a failure to get to a location on time. Remember, too, how important it is to keep the camera-operator informed. Say clearly what you expect, and although it is not necessary to know the technical details of every piece of equipment, a rudimentary understanding of and interest in how things work will contribute towards telling the story more effectively.

Meeting deadlines
Before satellites and microwave links became commonplace, news programmes relied on more basic forms of communication to ensure their raw material reached base in time for editing and transmission. The principle, if not the method, remains the same. Deadlines have shrunk, increasing pressure on the team in the field to plan their mission down to the finest detail. Calculations about the time needed to travel to and from the scene of a story, to gather the pictures and judge their worth, to shape the material on the spot or send the raw rushes to be edited at home base, plus a safety margin, have to be built into the schedule if programme requirements are to be met.

The whole process has been speeded up with the introduction of satellite news-gathering facilities and mobile edit suites, but the ability to control the logistical problems involved in reporting is valued almost as much as straightforward editorial talent.

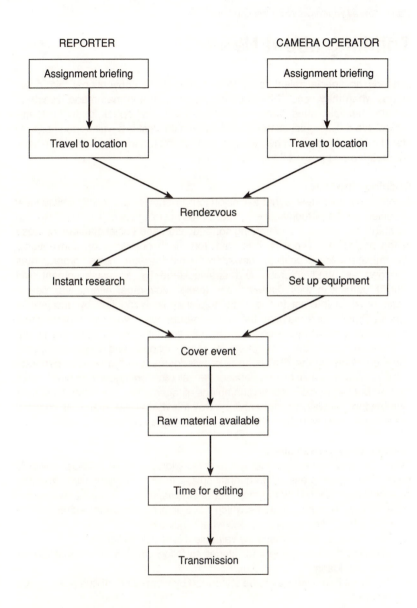

REPORTER	CAMERA OPERATOR
Assignment briefing	Assignment briefing
Travel to location	Travel to location

Rendezvous

| Instant research | Set up equipment |

Cover event

Raw material available

Time for editing

Transmission

Managing a news story
Whatever the assignment you must make a conscious effort to ensure all stages are completed so the material is ready to be broadcast by the programme for which it is intended. Allow sufficient leeway for your raw 'rushes' to be edited at base or assembled on the spot for 'live' transmission. Always build in a safety margin, especially abroad: it often takes longer to process the material than it does to gather it.

Don't allow all your news to be 'second hand'.

Thinking about News

It needs no special talent to be able to recognise conventional 'big' news stories when they occur. Political changes, natural and man-made disasters, social upheavals, unusual crimes, notable trials – all speak loudly for themselves. What distinguishes the journalist from the rest is a well-honed ability to identify the subjects which, although less obvious, stimulate interest or have real bearing on people's lives.

Opening 'The Gate'

A commonly held view is that television journalism offers a strictly limited view of society, and a parochial one at that. Some sociologists call it 'The Gate', an inevitable byproduct of the upbringing, education and social attitudes of those in the profession. There is, it is said, too much emphasis on conventional Westminster-based political news, with mainstream news programmes regarded as unadventurous and straitjacketed by an establishment and 'official' outlook in their domestic and foreign coverage. Alternative, 'democratic' news of interest to the wider audience is overlooked by accident or design. Other critics maintain the news agenda has always been determined by newspapers and television lacks the will and resources to break the mould.

To some extent the recruitment of more national and regionally based correspondents by the BBC is an acknowledgement of the need to generate more original journalism and reduce the reliance on agency-inspired news stories. But remember also the champions of 'alternative' news may have their own reasons for wishing to change the way television news makes its choices: not all have carry with them the burden of having to appear impartial.

Differences in news values

Television and newspaper journalists differ widely in their attitudes towards news. The tabloid press will frequently splash their front pages with offbeat or bizarre stories ignored by the more serious newspapers. Television will sometimes kick off with picture items which have little relevance for either print or sound. So how does anyone assess what is news?

- First, always ask yourself how valuable it is to the audience.
- Scouring the newspapers for stories to follow up is a poor substitute for your own ideas.
- Do not sit back and wait to be spoon-fed by what pours off the agency wire services.
- Get as close to the grass roots as possible in an attempt to generate original material.

Thinking about the news
Journalists differ widely in their attitudes. Newspapers aim their content at known socio-economic groups and don't rate subjects to which others give high priority.

Planning Future Coverage

Laypeople are commonly under the impression that 'news' consists entirely of unexpected and spectacular happenings in all parts of the world. This is not the case. Nor do television reporters go roaming the streets with their camera crews in search of news: it would be time-consuming and almost entirely non-productive. News gathering has to be approached on an organised and systematic basis. Professionally organised news services recognise this by dedicating teams of journalists to the filtering and discussion of ideas, building a catalogue of scheduled events at home.

This planning or futures desk – cornerstone of the intake or input department – is responsible for noting the dates of Parliamentary sessions, anniversaries, court sittings, the publication of official documents, and a wide range of other events which may be considered worthy of treatment by television.

Planners scour every newspaper and magazine that comes their way (the more obscure the better), watch other television programmes, listen to the radio, listen to gossip and rumour, and cultivate anyone who might provide a tip-off to a news story, in an effort to assemble the widest possible agenda from which a choice can be made.

The flow is two ways. Invitations to attend events are issued, facilities offered. On other occasions permission may have to be sought for reporters and camera crews to join private or public occasions, and then it is a matter of obtaining entry passes, security clearances or whatever documentation is required for access. Some really big events are arranged years in advance, and news organisations spend considerable time and effort to ensure they are represented, and have access to the proper communications and facilities.

Foreign news
Coverage of foreign news requires special attention, especially when reporters are assigned from their home base to cover stories. They may not be allowed to enter another country without a visa applied for several weeks ahead, and permission may have to be sought to take in a camera crew, customs declarations prepared, and official accreditation sought, all of which may take frustratingly long to arrange.

Regrettably few countries allow complete freedom of access to their own journalists, let alone to outsiders, and it is not unknown for planners to spend months unsuccessfully wooing those with the power to sanction such a visit. Quite often it is not so much what is happening in a country which is of interest to the outside world – simply that a closed or secretive society is for some reason prepared to open its doors briefly.

Future story sources

(including:
other media
own correspondents
unsolicited information
affiliates
'official' news
'events')

Planning ('futures')

Futures meetings

Daily diary

Assignment briefing

Pathway to the news
'News', however it is defined, comes from two main sources – the unexpected, 'breaking' stories, which tend to form a small proportion of the content of mainstream daily news programmes – and a range of known events for which coverage can be planned in advance. Story ideas for consideration follow an established pattern. Even those programmes or organisations with limited resources try to devote staff to essential planning duties. Any relationship between affiliated, local or regional television or radio stations multiplies sources and adds to news-gathering potential. Where radio and television operate side by side or in a genuine 'bi-media' environment, reporters may at times be called on to work in either discipline.

Assignment Planning

The second part of the planners' task is to assemble the list of story possibles into a suitable form for discussion at senior editorial level. These meetings are usually held at weekly or monthly intervals, the aim being to give programme editors sufficient time in which to evaluate everything being suggested. Some items are quickly discarded, others referred back for further invetigation before a decision is reached. For those that get the go-ahead, logistical problems may be considered briefly – perhaps the need for special travel arrangements, satellite bookings, co-operation with other departments or organisations – before detailed planning gets under way.

As a reporter you might not be involved at this early stage. It depends on the way your organisation works, whether news planning and news processing are separate or combined, and what ideas you have fed into the system.

The daily diary

Once reduced to manageable and unfanciful proportions, the original list of possibles becomes a declaration of commitment known as 'the diary' or 'the prospects', issued at the start of each working day. Now begins the detailed organisation of every story – at first sight a simple enough task, in reality often a slow, painstaking, frustrating experience. A planner's typical day might run thus:

- Arrange the collection of a long-awaited government publication in time for you to read, digest and turn into an item for the main news.
- Ensure that you and a camera crew, arriving separately from other duties, rendezvous at the same entrance of a building where an important interviewee can spare you exactly ten minutes.
- Find an official with the authority to open a security gate to allow the camera crew to drive within a short distance of where they need to set up their equipment.

This may seem to add up to a series of tedious chores far removed from journalism. But without it the document may not be read properly and an important angle missed; you and the crew may kick your heels at different entrances while the interviewee gives up and goes on to his next appointment without seeing you; the crew may have to carry their equipment half a kilometre from the public car park.

The assignments desk

Responsibility now shifts from the planners to the assigners – sometimes the same people, sometimes not. Reporters with known subject expertise are invariably allocated stories which make use of it. Briefing ranges from the cursory – not much more than subject heading, location and the name of a 'contact' – to the detailed discussion of treatment, content and the questions to be asked of interviewees.

Document 1:

CONFIDENTIAL: Strictly not for broadcast

Originator: JS: Feb 20 17:58

Home futures diary for March
==

Tuesday 7th:

Editors: Derek Ward, Kate Danziger, Sarah Yorke

Reporters on duty: Harry Hurst, Barry Leveton, Maureen Fra[n...]
David Blake (Bosnia)

Off duty: Pat Palmer, Carol Dobson

Duty lawyer:

CCI   Expected announcement of £8m expansion of elec[...]
             near Swindon. Prospect of 250 jobs. (ECONOMIC[...]
             ADVISE)

CRIME   Report on new trends. Home Office figures publi[...]
             news conference; Home Secretary available for in[...]
             Pre-filming of former crime blackspot in Manche[...]
             crewing.)

SCHOOLS   Teachers' unions combine to set out guidelines fo[...]
             maths and English standards. Possible Birmingh[...]

1

Document 2:

johnson Tue Mar 07 07:19   page 001
==============================STRICTLY NOT FOR BROADCAST==========

NEWS DIARY

EDITORS: Derek Ward, Kate Danziger, Sarah Yorke
CHIEF WRITER: Cynthia Greene   Tuesday March 07
PRESENTERS (a.m.) Rose Salter, Fred Goodwin
STUDIO DIRECTORS: Ilan Schindler, Carol Guest (p.m.) Richard Yoffey
NEWS EDITOR: Paul Zatz
DUTY LAWYER: Louise Gellman

REPORTERS ON DUTY: Harry Hurst, Barry Leveton, Maureen Franklin, Avril
Leon, David Blake (Bosnia)

OFF DUTY: Pat Palmer, Carol Dobson

HOME:

RAIL   Crash inquiry. Transport minister visits site (10.00) then to
             Royal Infirmary. Satlinks for Lunch News. (Hurst)

CCI   Announce £12 expansion of electronics factory
             near Swindon with 250+ jobs. Economics Correspondent plus
             pre-shot report.

CRIME   Report on new trends. Home Office figures published. London
             news conference; Home Secretary available for interview (a.m.)
             Pre-filming of former crime blackspot in Manchester (local
             crewing.)

PLAQUE   Unveiling of memorial to Tommy Thompson, rock star killed in
             motorway crash. Church service (1400) followed by formal
             dedication at Streatham house where he was born. Pool coverage

LOBBY   Students lobby over new Education Bill (Westminster, 1430)

HEALTH   Health minister at one day seminar, Warwick University.
             (Advance copy of speech available from News Desk on March 6

SOAPSTAR   Baby leaves hospital with proud parents. 1300? (Leon)

FOREIGN:

FISH   Euro debate on fish stocks, Strasbourg. French fishermen
             promising demonstrations, Paris and Calais

2

Document 3:

NEWSWATCH
Assignment Sheet
==

Date: 07.03

Assignment no: 471/009

Slug: Soapstar

Camera: Bryan

Reporter: Leon

Location:
     Main Hospital, Cuthbert Street, London N[...]

Time: 1400 approx.

Contact: Jean Stafford (Hospital admin) Phone[...]

Story details:
     The Soapstars are taking home their ne[...]

Coverage required:
     Exteriors hospital and waiting fans. Interviews with Soapstars if possible.
Shots of proud parents & offspring

Additional notes:
     Rendezvous 1245 James' cafe in Thomas Place (approx. 200 m from
hospital) Note: Balcony access possible through Jean Stafford.

Sheila Ansell
Duty News Editor

3

Story planning

Not all news is about unexpected events. Detailed planning of known happenings is
carried out well ahead. 'Futures' information (1) is distilled into Daily Diaries (2). The
Assignment Sheet (3) provides a basic briefing for reporter and camera crew.

Sources

Television news-related organisations are overwhelmed with unsolicited information which pours in from members of the public and with every mail delivery. In some cases it provides the backbone for programme coverage, but for the rest, existence without resort to some consistent professional back-up is likely to be regarded as scarcely possible.

The agencies

Much of the raw material on which news programmes are based comes fresh from the national and international wire services. The Press Association (PA) Reuters, the Associated Press (AP), United Press International (UPI), Agence France Press (AFP) and others like them provide a valuable subscription service of reports which appear on the video screens in newsrooms all over the world. Agency staff and freelance reporters are often the first to break stories, setting the pace for others to follow if they please.

Nearer home, each news desk has its own trusted sources to supplement the flow of intelligence from which the diaries are built up. The individual reporter – particularly the specialist – has the contacts book.

Making contact

People make news – so the name, address and telephone number of anyone who is or is ever likely to be of the slightest professional use should never be discarded. Those you come across may be previous interviewees, potential interviewees or providers of fact, record or opinion. Make a note of the officials of organisations which issue invitations or publicity handouts, local politicians and celebrities. Minor officials become major ones. Local politicians become national figures. Do not forget the expertise which is bound to exist within your own circle of friends, or the organisations to which you belong. Keep headed notepaper or visiting cards containing useful names and addresses.

Correspondence columns are also useful sources. A large proportion of letters comes from those who represent organisations of all types, and a surprising number of well-known people who hesitate to list their telephone numbers openly include their addresses when writing to newspapers. Keep a record of all those who might be of use.

Starting from scratch takes time, so at first it might be worth considering sharing names with others. Begin by swapping with a colleague of similar status. If you each concentrate on one subject area at a time you will make double the progress in half the time.

Keeping the list

Lastly, when you have built up your list, keep it safely. Experienced reporters guard their contacts books jealously. It may be worth putting yours in the bank when you go on holiday.

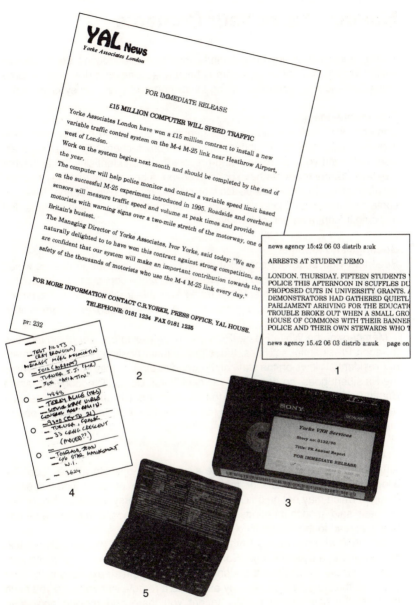

Sources

The wire services often provide the first indication of a breaking story (1). Modern distribution methods ensure the raw material is available on computer screens in the newsroom. Publicity handouts (2) remain regular sources of information sometimes worthy of being followed up for coverage. High-quality video news releases, produced to broadcast standard (3) are the visual equivalent. Good reporters build their own list of contacts and guard them jealously, whether they are kept in note-book style (4) or stored electronically in the memory of personal organisers (5).

Making Use of Your Contacts

Gossip and rumour are no substitute for fact, so it doesn't do to believe everything you are told. Scepticism is healthy as long as it does not become obsessive and blind you to accepting the evidence of your own eyes and ears.

The double-check
Contacts who seek you out may be genuinely anxious to help or may have their own axes to grind. It happens. If in doubt cross-check with other sources. Keep faith with your informants and respect their confidentiality if that is what they wish. Some reporters have gone to prison rather than reveal their sources of information. But be careful. Do not make promises you cannot keep. In some circumstances the act of receiving information can in itself be regarded as being in contravention of the law.

Briefings and lobbies
Reporters who deal with specialist subjects usually operate in groups which enjoy some privileges denied to generalists. Advance copies of official reports, speeches and other documents are made available to assist full and accurate reporting. Security passes and identity cards are issued to reporters with official accreditation.

Members of the White House Press Corps, for example, are given facilities to report Presidential activities. Aides give regular briefings – i.e. government or Presidential views on the state of the world or other issues of the day. Where the President goes, so does the President Press Corps. The lobby system in Britain enables political journalists to meet senior politicians and officials on a regular 'non-attributable' basis (see panel opposite), bringing with it the opportunity to discover current government thinking.

Uses and abuses
Although they have their uses, these systems are open to abuse. 'Lobbies' allow government officials or ministers to use the press to float ideas or theories which may not be official policy, and controversy over what has or has not been said at such meetings (which are never supposed to take place) has begun to lead to the discrediting of the whole idea.

Yet those who are barred from entry or refuse to take part sometimes find themselves at a disadvantage. Some stories are impossible to cover properly without 'official' help. Miss the plane to the President's next destination and you miss the story. You cannot buy a ticket to a remote war zone, so you have to enlist the help of the military to get you there and provide access to communications.

The trouble is that you will be taken subject to conditions imposed by your hosts – and in some cases that might be thought too high a price to pay.

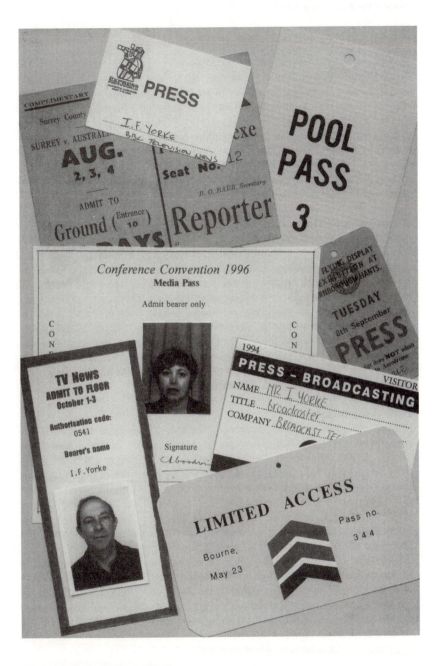

The passport to news coverage
Only bona fide journalists are admitted to most events likely to be worth covering.
Without prior accreditation, proper identification or official press pass you simply will not
be allowed access. Make sure you secure the right credentials, in good time.

Resisting Political Pressures

Despite their deep mutual distrust, journalists and politicians in the United Kingdom have come to co-exist in the knowledge that they need each other. Yet the perceived influence of the media – especially television – on public opinion, particularly at election times, and the increasingly 'presidential' nature of party politics, has led to unprecedented, unrelenting and sometimes crude pressure by politicians or their supporters on journalists carrying out their duties. Your role as a reporter is not to be deflected from seeking and broadcasting the truth as you see it. In the hot-house atmosphere of modern newsgathering this can be extremely difficult.

Defending against 'the spin'
Politicians and other public figures pursue publicity in their attempts to get their message across. To help them the main players now employ propagandists, 'media specialists' or 'image consultants', whose role includes trying to put the most favourable gloss on news stories which on the surface might not appear to be to their advantage.To the journalists they are known as 'spin doctors', and their attempts at exploiting the news media have become a significant factor in the coverage of modern political news. It is not all one-sided: journalists are ever on the lookout for the smallest signs of individual financial or sexual peccadillos, Government splits or factional in-fighting and the by-play between the two sides has taken on the appearance of a game in which the participants constantly try to outwit each other.

Video news releases
The ready availability of broadcast standard camera equipment has spawned the birth of the Video News Release, a visual version of the written press release. VNRs, often produced to the same high quality of the mainstream news programmes are provided free (usually) by specialist or public relations companies, and contain attractive raw news material which might not be available under any other circumstances. For hard-pressed news organisations with rarely enough resources to cover every news item they would like, readymade VNR material is often as innocuous and informative as it is useful, but journalists should treat it as they would any other press release. 'Wall-paper' pictures of otherwise inaccessible locations or commercial production processes may be all very well, but journalists should be suspicious of executives who prefer to be interviewed 'in-house' rather than risk exposure to outsiders. At times, also, the nature and content of VNRs offered by pressure groups can appear almost irresistible, but the makers' own agenda and the material itself should always be scrutinised with great care before a decision is made whether to allow any of it on-screen.

ON THE RECORD means what you are told is for broadcast or publication.
● No problem, subject to legal constraints.

OFF THE RECORD means what you are told is not for broadcast or publication.
● More of a problem. Try to establish in advance how much of the information you *can* use. Don't agree to the condition retrospectively without very serious consideration.

NOT FOR ATTRIBUTION means you can broadcast or publish what you are told as long as you do not reveal the source of the information.
● Very much a problem. Sometimes used in an attempt at news management. Be wary.

LOBBY BRIEFINGS are usually for groups of specialist journalists by invitation from government or other official sources. Information may be given only on a non-attributable basis.
● Can be a problem. If you join a lobby you must expect to abide by its rules.

ACCREDITATION gives limited numbers of journalists access to places or events where official information is made available.
● Ditto. Being accredited is sometimes the only way of getting to a story.

EMBARGOES allow journalists to have advance copies of documents, reports, speeches or other information on the understanding that broadcast or publication will not take place until a given time.
● Useful but sometimes contentious. Treat every embargo on its merits and be alert to the possibility of news manipulation. Always check advance copies of speeches against delivery: there is no guarantee against a speaker departing from a prepared text.

NEWS BLACKOUTS are sought by the authorities when they believe broadcast or publication could endanger life.
● Acceptable only under certain conditions usually decided at high level. Never commit yourself. Always refer such requests to senior colleagues.

REQUESTS FOR ANONYMITY are made by people who believe broadcast or publication would be harmful.
● Treat with caution. There are circumstances in which anonymity should be granted: make no promises and refer to senior colleagues.

Seeing How It's Done (1)

In the absence of a structured induction, this suggested pattern is intended to provide newcomers with a basic understanding how a reporter fits into a news organisation. As every television station is organised differently, no more than a general guide can be offered, so use your initiative to adapt the programme to suit your own circumstances.

Try to carry out all the stages over a concentrated period of a week, but if this is not possible follow through on successive duty days. The programme assumes the willingness of others to let you observe them at close quarters. It is possible you may be thrown in at the deep end without the opportunity to learn from others, but if you get the chance – take it.

Stage 1: Planning and assignments
Sit with those responsible for sifting through ideas for coverage. Helping to answer the telephone or open the mail will give you a feel for the range of material which comes up for consideration. Judge for yourself what is newsworthy and compare the decisions taken by those doing the job for real. Go to planning meetings which discuss the details of future assignments. See how stories are graded in importance and the extent to which reporters are briefed before they embark on projects. Listen to the communications between reporters in the field and producers/editors back at base. Assess the accuracy, quality, frequency and amount of information on offer. If necessary, determine to improve it when your turn comes.

Stage 2: On the road
Accompany a reporter colleague and camera operator on assignment, preferably one which needs thought and careful planning rather than a straight hard news story requiring little finesse. Stay and observe until the end, no matter how tedious it might become. Make a note of the order in which the reporter tackles the various ingredients and how well or badly he or she treats interviewees, contacts and others involved. If the opportunity arises ask to use the camera yourself: 'multi-skilling' is becoming widespread and the sooner you are able to gain an understanding of other roles you may play in future, the better.

Stage 3: Picture editing
Follow 'your' story into the edit suite and watch the picture editor assemble it. Ask if you can carry out a simple 'hands-on' exercise. If possible spend time with more than one editor: get an idea of their routines and contrast their styles. Is one a quicker worker than others? What shots are they inclined to discard? Are they led by the strength of the pictures or sound? Do they slavishly follow instructions or do they use their imagination? At what point, if any, does editorial supervision take place?

Stage 1:
Planning and
assignments (courtesy
BBC Central Stills)

Stage 2:
On the road

Stage 3:
Picture editing

Watching brief (1)
If necessary give up your spare time to watch what happens at each stage. It will
provide a valuable insight into the editorial process and help you develop your own
approach to working relationships. Changes in technology and working practices may
mean you have to operate the camera or edit your own pictures, so seek practical,
'hands-on' experience if the opportunity arises.

Watching Brief (2)

The second part of your watching brief should concentrate on production and technical areas.

Stage 4: Graphics
Follow the activities of one graphics designer over the course of the whole day. Is one programme served, or are there several 'customers', each requiring a different style? Make sure you understand the system. Is instruction given verbally, or is there a more formal procedure? Are ideas for graphics generated by reporters or other journalists for the artist to follow, or vice versa? Time how long it takes to create each graphic and note the periods of the day when pressure of work seems greatest. Ask who is responsible for checking the accuracy of graphics designs – particularly figures and spellings – against original ideas and completed scripts. On transmission, make a particular point of judging whether there is a real match between the graphic and the accompanying commentary. If there is little or none, find out why.

Stage 5: The newsroom
Observe a newswriter or item producer at work on your chosen programme and monitor every stage of the process. Get an idea of what sources are used, particularly those which are considered reliable and those which are not. Note how much of the script is the writer's own words and how much is a straight crib from wire copy. Pay special attention to the writer's working relationships with programme editor, reporter and picture editor working on the same story, and how much influence is brought to bear by others. Be there when the running order/rundown is constructed. Try to understand why items are shortened or dropped. Stay for the programme post mortem, if there is one.

Stage 6: Studio and production
Follow the studio director as preparations are made to put the programme on the air. Sit in on script or technical conferences and listen to what is said about journalistic performances. Watch the rehearsal, however sketchy it might be. Evaluate the director's performance under the pressure of a live newscast. Spend some time in the studio, where you can judge whether the floor manager gives clear signals and whether the script-prompting operation is effective.

Stage 7: Practice
By the time you have reached Day 7 your colleagues will have decided you are a perfectionist or a plain nuisance. Either way, persuade them to give you some reading practice during studio downtime. A script from a previous transmission will suffice. Use the electronic prompting device, if there is one. Then ask for an honest opinion.

Stage 4: Graphics
(courtesy Quantel)

Stage 5: Newsroom
(courtesy Sky News)

Stage 6: Production
(courtesy BBC
Central Stills)

Stage 7: Practice
(courtesy EDS
Portaprompt)

Watching brief (2)
The second half of the programme concentrates on production and technical areas.
You should end up with a full understanding of how your organisation works and your
part in it.

Make the Most of Your Talent

Television reporters are expected to be bright, eager, inquisitive and persistent. These are the minimum qualities you should already possess before beginning to develop 'performing' skills for the screen. Nothing can be achieved without them, so make sure they come across – to your producer or programme editor, to those you deal with every day in the pursuit of your journalism and, above all, to your audience. Understand every story before you embark on it. Make use of any background material which might prove helpful. Think. Be informed: there is nothing worse than a reporter who is made to look foolish by an interviewee because of his or her own ignorance. Read a variety of newspapers and magazines. Watch television, especially your own output and that of your closest competition. Listen to and master the basics of radio journalism – you may find yourself working in a 'bi-media' environment where you are expected to be expert in both disciplines. Learn keyboard skills – few self-respecting newsrooms are without computers. Be sure you can drive, if that is appropriate for where you intend to work. Be interested in everything from sport to politics. Learn another language. Who knows when it might lead to a glamorous foreign assignment?

Style and 'presence'
The qualities which add up to an acceptable screen 'presence' are in themselves subjective and almost impossible to define. It is easier to identify the negative. The camera is a cruel exposer of physical peculiarities and mannerisms, and the microphone exaggerates speech defects. Even so, every editor has a different idea of what personality is suitable for his or her programme. Voice and 'looks' also come into it because, like it or not, there is no escaping human nature. But a pretty or handsome face is not enough. Fashions change, sometimes driven by the technology which creates demands for different skills.

At one time television news seemed to be peopled entirely by solemn, mature males with greying hair. Then came an explosion in opportunities for women and those from ethnic minority backgrounds. The biggest change of all has seen the replacement of the news 'reader' by the news 'presenter' or 'caster', an experienced journalist able to deal with a growing proportion of live interviews and other material within fast-moving programmes.

The need for training
Try at the outset to get a realistic assessment of your talents. It may be hurtful to be told you have an inherent weakness of voice, for example, which may never be overcome, but it is better than holding out unreasonable expectations. The main reporting techniques, including writing and interviewing, can usually be acquired with proper training. Technique can be picked up simply 'sitting by Nellie', but Nellie may have learned the same way and may have developed bad habits of her own.

Section 1: Essential

(a) Writing ability

(b) Intelligence

(c) Inquisitiveness

(d) Persistence

(e) Strong interest in current events

Section 2: Expected

(a) Ability to 'fit in'

(b) Ideas

(c) Knowledge of specialist subject

(d) Second language

Section 3: Tools of the trade

(a) Keyboard skills/computer skills

(b) Driving

(c) Shorthand

Section 4: Broadcasting qualities

(a) Speech clarity

(b) Speech tone

(c) Screen 'presence'

Check your own skills
Check off your skills in the boxes provided. At the very least you should have positive answers to all of Section 1.

Wear the right clothes for the right occasion.

Dressing the Part (1)

The attention lavished by members of the viewing public and the newspaper industry on those who appear regularly on the television screen has developed into something approaching an international pastime. Such is the level of interest, gossip and comment, it has become possible to believe that discussion about almost any night's television news centres as much on what the main female presenter was wearing – and speculation as to what it might have cost – as on programme content.

Keeping the audience's attention

Dress should not be important, but it is, because an audience concentrating on a frilly blouse, a plunging neckline or a tie with a curious motif will be distracted from what is being said. And that audience, once distracted, is lost to the reporter and the programme. So it is essential that what the reporter/presenter wears is both unremarkable and appropriate for the occasion. Extrovert clothes may be acceptable for a programme aimed at a teenage or fashion-conscious audience, not for the main mid-evening news. While a safari-style suit may look right for reporting from the scene of a jungle war, it would scarcely do for conducting a formal studio interview with a leading politician. Similarly, the 'office' suit and tie is out of place in the jungle. In both cases, common sense and good manners will offend neither the interviewee nor the viewer, who in most countries is surprisingly easily offended by lapses from what he or she understands as accepted standards of behaviour.

Programme dress rules

Programmes sometimes impose their own styles of dress on their performers as part of a co-ordinated 'look' intended to create the overall tone they wish to impart to the viewer: for example, reporters and presenters on breakfast shows may be required to wear sweaters or other casual clothes to fit in with the easy chairs and coffee tables surrounding them on the set; an evening news programme may seek to create an entirely different atmosphere by putting its talent into more formal wear and an austere set; others are known to make it mandatory for on-screen performers to wear company 'uniform', and so on. At the same time, common sense dictates that a reporter arriving first at the scene of a major breaking news story should not risk missing it by taking time to change into programme-style clothes.

If the reporter does not have a firm set of 'dress-on-duty' rules to go by – and this probably applies to the majority – the one infallible guideline is simply to dress in a way which does not invite notice. Keep the eye-catching items for off-duty days.

1

2

3

4

Dress

Clothes should match the mood of the programme and assignment.
1. The reporter covering a story in the jungle looks right in a bush shirt.
2. But formal wear is more appropriate for the studio ...
3. ... especially when the interviewee is 'correctly' dressed.
4. The wrong choice can create embarrassment all round.

Dressing the Part (2)

There are other problems connected with wearing the right clothes for the right occasion, because the television studio imposes some disciplines of its own. The sensitive mechanism inside electronic colour cameras can be disturbed by fine stripes or check patterns, triggering a visual vibration known as 'strobing'. Pointing the camera at some colours – notably some shades of blue – creates an electronic hole through which the studio background appears. An occasional check with programme technical or production staff will help to avoid any of these embarrassments.

Accessories
The same care should be taken with accessories: shiny jewellery can reflect studio lighting and create irritating 'flare'. Long, dangling ropes of beads, bracelets and suchlike tend to have minds all of their own in the studio or on location, and are a sure way of attracting the wrong attention – especially when they sway in the wind, become entangled in the microphone lead, or fall off.

Hairstyles
Much the same approach should be taken with hairstyles. Anything unusual is almost certain to come between the reporter's words and the audience, who are equally quick to spot changes of style or colour. For males and females alike, the best is an easily manageable combination of neatness and simplicity.

Beards
Some news programmes go to extremes and simply ban their regular male performers from the screen if they have beards or moustaches, but even those who do not usually have a sensible rule: consistency. A bearded man who suddenly appears clean-shaven is going to present viewers with an identity crisis long enough to spoil his first story or two.

Cosmetics
During the early days of television, anyone appearing before the studio camera wore make-up which resembled that used by circus clowns – white faces and green or blue lipstick. The sensitivity of modern television equipment means that nature requires little embellishment for those involved in daily factual programmes. Normal, everyday cosmetics are perfectly acceptable for females. Male faces may need only a light dusting of powder to take the shine off foreheads and noses under the studio lights, and the application of a light foundation cream will mask a 'five o'clock shadow' if shaving is not possible before a programme.

Skin tones vary, of course, so it makes sense to know what makeup is most suitable personally and to keep it handily placed for use with the minimum of delay when necessary.

1

2

3

4

Some unexpected problems
1. Check patterns and some stripes cause 'strobing'.
2. Jewellery reflects in studio lighting and causes 'flare'.
3. Be consistent with hairstyle and colouring.
4. Viewers notice even subtle changes in the appearance of their favourite regular performers.

Voice Production

With the 'look' goes the voice – and probably just as much controversy. Certainly in British broadcasting the idea of what speech is 'acceptable' has changed dramatically over the past thirty years. Before then it was rare to hear any regular broadcaster who did not speak with the tone and accent closely associated with the south-east of England. Since then the arrival of local radio and television has produced a wider variety of regional accents, allowing viewers to identify more comfortably with broadcasters from their own area. Whether this has contributed to the drastic drop in the standards of language usage is entirely subjective.

The wish to communicate

Although almost any voice will improve with training, not every one will be suitable for broadcasting. The main thing for the beginner is to *want* to communicate. This means writing for speech in a way which comes across to the listener as natural. Sentences should be constructed so proper phrasing is possible, because that in turn will aid the audience's comprehension. The second priority is to ensure the words, once written, are delivered with a reasonable range of inflection. Some voices are naturally monotonous, but to make matters worse many young reporters develop a tendency to speak quickly in a flat undertone they think adds a sense of urgency to their work. In general the more nervous the speaker, the higher the pitch, so although it is by no means easy, the reporter must allow his or her muscles to relax so the full tonal range comes through. The listener relies on the clarity of the speech as much as on the power of the pictures, and the reporter who speaks poorly is doing only half the job.

Appointments procedures for reporters often include a rigorous voice test, and those who have been found to have lisps, other speech impediments or impenetrable accents have been denied the jobs their otherwise excellent journalistic pedigree deserved. Some speech deficiencies can be cured with practice or the attention of therapists: the viewer should be spared the rest.

Pronunciation

Another essential ingredient of the voice-and-speech process is pronunciation. This is often a matter of editorial policy rather than individual taste, because the audience needs to be sure a name or place mentioned in last night's news is in fact the same as that repeated by someone else from the same programme tonight or tomorrow. The biggest news organisations have sophisticated methods to aid this consistency. The BBC supplies its broadcasters regularly with updates of 'difficult' names and places in the news, supplementing this with additional information when international conferences, the Olympics, or similarly lengthy events occur. Not every broadcaster can afford to go that far, so dictionaries of pronunciation, a good memory and a home-made index based on experience can be made just as effective.

VOICE-OVER FOR MINISTER'S VISIT

ENG AIRPORT   Several *hundred* demonstrators were waiting for the Minister's arrival. But police made sure they were kept at the far end of the airport, well away from the VIP reception area. *Whatever the protesters believe*, the two governments have publicly stated their intention of improving relations between them: the Minister's arrival is seen as an important first step.

CAR LEAVES   *This evening* the Minister is due to pay a courtesy call on the President. The Two sides get down to business proper at the Foreign Ministry first thing tomorrow morning. The Minister will be here for the next four days. During that time he is expected to meet leaders of the main *Opposition* parties as well as senior members of the Government.

Voice production

Write as for speech, keeping sentences short. This combined with simple, everyday language, will help make delivery seem more natural. When setting out voice-over scripts try to remember the convention that text appears on the right and production/technical instructions on the left. Mark words or phrases to help with intonation.

Speech Clarity

Successful voice production also depends on body posture and proper breathing control. Consult a voice trainer or speech therapist if you can afford it: any such lessons will be an investment in your future career. They will be well worth the financial sacrifice and are probably tax-deductible anyway.

If you are left to your own devices, read some of the many books on the subject, and make use of modern technology.

Try reading your scripts into a tape recorder and be as honestly critical as possible of the results when playing them back. Don't cheat by referring to the original material. Put it aside and listen carefully, making sure you have understood every word you have said. If not, practise until it sounds right.

A second stage might be to use a home video camera to reveal other possible faults. Some readers are surprised to discover they close or screw up their eyes when faced with unfamiliar words or pronunciation.

Whatever method you decide to use, do not be afraid to experiment with 'difficult' readings. Mastery of a range of material will give you confidence, and if you detect problems seek expert advice as soon as possible.

No smoking rules

Those who use their voice professionally should smoke very little or not at all. Michael McCallion, who taught voice at the Royal Academy of Dramatic Art and whose work includes helping actors, pop singers, and politicians in many parts of the world, also believes heavy spirit drinking should be avoided (*The Voice Book*: see page 168). It is better not to drink alcohol at all before a reading performance, so when pre-programme courtesies are being extended, keep off the gin, and stick to the tonic.

Conquering stage fright

In your early days of television reporting – whether it is on location or in the studio – nerves are bound to affect your work. Symptoms include chest tightness, faster beating of the heart, and a dry throat and mouth.

It can become a vicious circle: if you seem too nervous on screen, editors may not be prepared to risk putting you on; the less you appear, the more your confidence drains; the less confidence you have, the more nervous you will become, and so on.

The answer is to offer to do anything which will diminish your fear of the microphone. Reading off-camera voice-overs and programme 'trailers' may not be the same as full-scale reporting, but they do allow the use of your voice in public performance.

Common faults in speech
Monotonous delivery
Voice trails away at end of sentence
Difficulties in saying 'r', 's', 'v', 'w'
Emphasis on wrong word
Emphasis on wrong syllable
Final consonants missing, especially the 'g' in '–ing'
Opening letter 'h' dropped

Words commonly mispronounced

	instead of	
amblence		ambulance
(l) arst		asked
Antartic		Antarctic
Artic		Arctic
Austrailyer		Australia
confrence		conference
crear		career
drogatry		derogatory
edyucashun		education
economickle		economical
Febery/Febury		February
Guvna (Prison)		Governor
Hospitawl/Hospitorl		hospital
ishoo		issue
Janury		January
jewring		during
jool (robbery)		jewel
Krea (North or South)		Korea
lible (to flooding)		liable
manidgement (and unions)		management
nachral (environment)		natural
nooclear		nuclear
noos (good or bad)		news
pleece		police
Pryminister		Prime Minister
saterlite		satellite
Secertry (Defence/Home)		secretary
sprise (announcement)		surprise
tempracher/temprachure		temperature
thee		the
twenny		twenty
uszul		usual
vilence		violence
wevver		weather/whether
wiv		with
yesterdee		yesterday

'Tell' your story to one viewer.

A Friend in the Audience

Try not to think of the audience in millions or thousands. That is far too terri-
fying a prospect. It will help your confidence to find a more realistic model. If
the 'man in the street' is too abstract a concept, aim what you do at someone
you know: a friend or family member, sitting at home on their own. Forget the
camera. Instead, try to imagine you are telling your story to them alone. Try to
gauge their reaction to what you are saying and how you are saying it.

Be logical
Remember that whatever you do, 'your' viewer sees it only once – and not
always under the best conditions and with full concentration. Research
suggests that audience comprehension of television news programmes is
often very poor, even within the most sophisticated societies. Viewing is
frequently interrupted, and those watching are known to be easily distracted.
They misunderstand and confuse even simple stories, let alone the more
abstract issues in a highly complex modern world. Help them. Make your
reports for the audience, not your boss or the critics. Be logical. Use clear,
direct language that everyone can understand. But do not patronise or insult
the intelligence of the better-educated.

Develop a rapport
The best reporters have a rapport with their audience in a way which tran-
scends gender or race. These are the people who inform nations about
matters of seriousness and importance. As such they are welcomed into every
living room every evening. They seem trustworthy and honest: that is why so
many are sought after to appear in commercials.

Who are they? Walter Cronkite of CBS was regularly voted the most trusted
man in America. The big names of the late 1990s crop up regularly in discussion inside and outside television journalism. The spread and speed of the
global communications satellite system has added an international dimension
to the work of Kate Adie, Michael Buerk, Michael Nicholson, Peter Jennings,
Trevor MacDonald, John Suchet and many others. Watch them closely and
see what makes them special.

Learn from others
Study your peers – especially those you admire – and try to understand them.
Without consciously copying, learn from their obvious strengths and apparent
weaknesses. Do not be afraid of changing your style more than once until you
feel comfortable with what you are doing. If necessary, ask others for their
opinions. You will soon learn to identify those whose judgement you can trust.

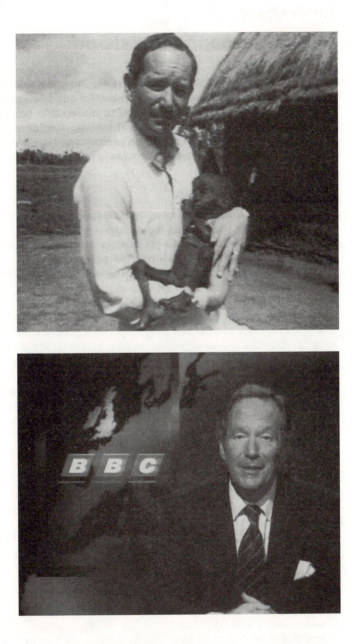

Role models
Thanks to the development of satellite communications technology Michael Buerk of the BBC has been one of the internationally known names of TV journalism for the past fifteen years. He has won awards for his reporting of events in Ethiopia and South Africa and has since brought his experience to the screen as a news presenter. (courtesy BBC Central Stills)

Simplicity rules.

How to Write for Television

In recognising the power of television pictures it is easy to undervalue the importance of the accompanying words. Yet the need for good writing has never been greater. Audiences are being asked to understand political, social, economic and environmental issues which will fundamentally affect their lives in the closing years of the 20th century and beyond. As a television reporter you will fail if what you provide is not comprehensible to ordinary people.

Keep it simple
Despite the welcome development of news-related programmes dealing with specialist subjects, most television journalism is aimed at a general audience. Unlike newspapers, able to target readership precisely according to socio-political groupings, television has to appeal to and be understood by all, so it must neither be too intellectual nor insult the intelligence. Your main aim must be to tell your stories in language which is: ● Accurate ● Clear ● Simple ● Direct ● Neutral.

Write as you speak
Something strange comes over many otherwise good journalists when they write for television. Clear thoughts become cluttered and confused, simple sentences convoluted. Direct language translates into 'officialese'.

The rule is: *think before you write*. Better still: *think aloud before you write*. The less natural it sounds, the more likely it is to be wrong. When did you last hear someone in the course of normal conversation say: 'I see the government is proposing a one billion pound cash boost for the National Health Service?' You might have heard 'I see the government's going to give the National Health Service more money. It's a billion pounds.'

Be logical
● Where possible, tell stories chronologically.
● As a general rule try to make it one short sentence, one thought.
● Understand what you are writing: if you don't, no-one will.
● Don't be put off by the language of official documents. Sometimes they are written deliberately to confuse or obfuscate, but more often the writer has no feeling for words.
● Always ask yourself: what am I trying to say? Then say it.

Avoid stupidities
Mistakes are made by reporters blind to the context of their words. Unintentional double-entendres, carelessness or insensitivities creep into broadcast material. Be alive to the changes in word usage. For example, 'gay' has a modern meaning far removed from its once better-known definition of joyful or light-hearted.

Reporter-speak

Language should be kept clear, simple, direct and accurate. Avoid stock phrases and clichés and stupidities. The list below is merely a taster ...

A (one-hundred-year-old vase) comes under the auctioneer's hammer ...	going, going, gone – for good!
Ambulances rushed ...	do they ever dawdle?
... biggest manhunt since ...	... the last biggest manhunt
Decimate ...	... means one in ten
Every available man ...	unavailable man couldn't be there could he?
Full-scale (inquiry/search) ...	are they ever anything less?
Fulsome praise/tribute ...	nearly always used incorrectly. It means insincere
Flames/smoke rose fifty/a hundred feet/miles ...	only if it's not just guesswork
Gunned down ...	ugh!
Helping the police with their inquiries :	euphemism interpreted as meaning the miscreant has been caught. Not always the case.
It's being said/called/people say ...	reporter-speak for your own opinion
Legendary figure of the decade ...	legends aren't created that quickly
... (more increases) in the pipeline ...	keep it to gas or oil
Road blocks were set up ...	it's routine
The explosion was heard ...	see flames/smoke
What impact has this had on the town?	question asked at the time of the Lockerbie air disaster of 1988

Reporter-speak openers	Reporter-speak closers
Here behind/in front of me ...	... is anyone's guess
I'm standing ...	... only time will tell
It happened ...	... will never be the same again
Security was strict/tight ...	... too little, too late
The lights are burning late ...	

Good Language

The drive for reporters to use direct, conversational language does not mean that sloppiness is acceptable. What is wanted is the most appropriate and accurate word. Unfortunately, many which trip off the average writer's word processor are chosen without much thought as to their meaning.

Anyone who has the temerity to offer advice to others on the use of language is asking for trouble. But it is worth the risk to point out that it does no journalist harm to refresh the memory from time to time. For those who take pride in what they do there are many excellent reference books, from the learned to the down-to-earth, offering guidelines on structure, definitions and grammar.

Slang
The line between colloquial language and slang is a thin one, easily crossed. The distinction is made all the more difficult because the word or expression frowned on yesterday becomes absorbed into normal speech patterns today, and becomes a dictionary entry tomorrow. My advice is to be cautious – let the lexicographers set the pace.

Eponyms
Where would we be without (the 4th Earl of) Sandwich, (Anders), Celsius, (Captain Charles) Boycott, (André) Amp(ère) and the rest who gave their names to household words? But there is a difference between eponyms and trade names. Not every vacuum cleaner is a (William) Hoover, nor every ball-point pen a (Laszlo) Biro. Legal actions have been fought over careless uses which have brought trade names of products into disrepute.

Clichés
There is a long list of stock phrases kept by journalists in their writing armouries. Not that they necessarily like using them – journalists make jokes against themselves about news stories composed entirely of clichés, and would much prefer to invent elegant alternatives. Those given to the occasional lapse under pressure can be forgiven: for the rest, a close scrutiny of *Roget's Thesaurus* is strongly recommended.

Acronyms
These constitute a form of jargon. Some have passed into the language as dictionary entries, NATO and the UN among them. But they need to be understood by the writer. In military parlance the acronym SAM, for example, is short for 'surface-to-air missile' – so to describe it as a 'SAM missile' is in fact saying 'surface-to-air missile missile'. Similarly, in Britain, the 'M1': in this context 'M' stands for motorway – so to describe the 'M1' as the 'M1 motorway' is saying 'motorway-1 motorway'.

Generic terms are preferable to trade names. They avoid giving free advertising, and misuse has been known to lead to legal action. Common examples appear below.

Trade names	Generic term
Airwick	air-freshener
Aladdin	oil-heater, oil-lamp
Ansafone	telephone answering machine
Ascot	gas water heater
Autocue	television script prompter
Band-aid	first aid dressing/plaster
Bic/Biro	ballpoint pen
Black and Decker	power tool
Caterpillar	tractor
Catseye	reflective road marker/stud
Cellophone	transparent wrapping
Coca-cola, Coke	cola, soft drink
Dictaphone	dictating machine
Dormobile	minibus
Elastoplast	first-aid dressing/plaster
Fibreglass	glass fibre
Formica	plastic laminate
Frigidaire	refrigerator
Gallup Poll	opinion poll
Harpic	lavatory cleaner
Hoover	vacuum cleaner
Jacuzzi	whirlpool bath
Jeep	field car
Kleenex	(paper) tissue
Land-Rover	four-wheel drive
Lego	plastic building bricks
Letraset	instant/rub-on lettering
Levi's	jeans
Li-lo	airbed
Perspex	acrylic sheet
Photostat	photocopy
Plasticine	modelling clay
Polaroid	instant picture
Portacabin	portable building
Primus	camping lamp/stove
Range-Rover	four-wheel drive
Rawlplug	wallplug
Scotch Tape	sticky tape
Sellotape	sticky tape
Singer	sewing machine
Tannoy	public address (system)
Tarmac	apron (for example)
Teasmade	automatic tea-maker
Thermos	vacuum flash
Triplex	safety glass
Underseal	rubberised coating
Vynolay	vinyl flooring
Xerox	photocopy

Words take on new meanings with common usage.

Avoiding Unnecessary Offence

Any heightened awareness of the importance of accurate English must take account of the need to avoid sexist, racist or other language likely to cause offence.

Sexism
Words which fail to recognise the proper place of women in modern society are offensive, especially when there are neutral alternatives. Sexist language is also often inaccurate. Progress towards its elimination is being made, particularly in the United States and Western Europe, although there is still a long way to go, and resistance to some of the alternatives which the more conservative members of the older generation especially find difficult to accept. As a reporter you should make a conscious decision to use gender-free words without going so far the other way that you will alienate the rest of the audience.

Racism
In the multicultural democracies of the 1990s, the careless or unwitting use of racist language is unforgivable. It is not usually necesary to refer to someone's colour, religion or racial origins, so unless it adds materially to the understanding of the story, don't.

It is also astonishing how ignorant some journalists are about the world's main religious beliefs (including their own, if they have them). Classic errors include references to 'Jewish churches', a complete under-estimation of the importance of Islam and Buddhism, and confusion about the titles of religious leaders. Most faiths have public relations officers or their equivalent: ask them to clarify for the sake of accuracy.

Ageism
The newspaper obsession with giving the ages of virtually all those they feature is fortunately not as prevalent in broadcast journalism. The test should always be whether the inclusion of someone's age will help the audience towards a better understanding of the story.

Political labels
Labels can be extremely useful. 'Right-wing' or 'far-left', for example, are short-hand idications of the views of political figures, and an attempt to put them into context. At times they can be more misleading than helpful, because those to whom the label is applied might not agree that it is an accurate reflection of where they stand in the political spectrum. Someone described as being on 'the left wing of the Labour Party' might object on the grounds that their views are left-wing only in comparison with those colleagues who have adopted what appears to them to be more 'right-wing' policies. So think carefully before using a political label which might be contentious. Or spend a few extra words getting it absolutely right.

AVOIDING UNNECESSARY OFFENCE

Be aware of the sensitivities of others. Sexist language, for example, will often be inaccurate as well. The list below is a guide to some of the alternatives. It is not meant to be complete or definitive – or cause offence itself.

Words	... and better words
Businessman	business people
Chairman/woman	(in the) chair, chaired by, presided over
Clergyman	cleric, clergy
Convict	inmate, prisoner
Cripples	people with disabilities
Fireman	fire-fighter
Fisherman	angler
Freshmen	freshers/first-years
Gentleman's agreement	verbal agreement
Girl	woman (unless a child)
Her/him/hers/his	their, theirs
Ladies	women
Laymen	laity, lay people
Mankind	humanity, people
Man-hours	work-hours
Man-made	artificial, hand-made, manufactured
Man-to-man	one-to-one
Manned	crewed, staffed
Manpower	staff, workers, workforce
Man-powered	human-powered
Negro	Afro-American, Afro-Caribbean, black, etc.
Newsman	journalist, reporter
Nightwatchman	caretaker, security guard
Old	elderly
One man, one vote	one person, one vote
Policeman	police officer
Spaceman	astronaut
Spokesman	official, representative
Sportsmen	sports people, contestants, competitors
Statesman	diplomat, politician, etc.
Stewardess	cabin crew/staff, flight attendant
Warder	prison officer
Workmen	workers, workforce

Aiming for Comprehension

Experimental sessions conducted under conditions in which there are no distractions prove the comprehension levels of audiences watching television news to be depressingly low.

Many viewers have great difficulty in recalling the content of programmes they have only just witnessed, are unable to remember in detail what individual stories were about, confuse the identities of personalities and mix up geographical locations.

Neither are matters helped by the professionals' own disinclination to allow for the circumstances in which their programmes are normally viewed. They forget that interruptions of all sorts impinge upon the concentration of even the most sophisticated audiences, who are probably only half-listening anyway.

Keep in touch

There is a broadcast journalist's adage which goes: 'Say what you are going to say; say it; then say what you have said.' That has become perhaps too simplistic, but it remains a useful reminder of the reporter's priority aim – to keep in touch with the audience. What you write must be easy on the ear, understandable at the first – and presumably only – hearing, with the story as a whole built up progressively in sequence.

Signposting

Unlike the reader of a newspaper, who has come to expect the Who, What, Where and When of every story to be packed into every opening sentence, the viewer is denied the luxury of a second glance. The first duty of the writer is to tune in the audience mentally by use of a 'signpost'. This device is especially useful as an introduction to a story, or as a means of indicating a change of pace, subject or idea, as it is intended to delay the most important information just long enough for the viewer to register the context.

'Signposts' do not need to consist of more than a short phrase or word or two, especially when they are used in the body of a story. They should not be falsely contrived, but their use should be developed consciously by every writer as part of story construction technique.

Facts and figures

Don't be guilty of assault by detail. Trade and budget figures, the fluctuations of currencies, stocks and shares – statistics of any sort – are notoriously difficult to get across with real clarity. As a general rule it is easier to take in figures as round numbers, so it is far better, for example, to describe the monthly total of unemployed as being 'nearly two million' instead of 'one million, eight hundred and fifty four thousand, six hundred and twelve'. Leave the full details for any accompanying graphics.

Signposts
Crucial facts are easily missed by viewers, particularly at the beginning of news stories. Carefully chosen signpost words or phrases will alert them to what they are about to hear or see.

Signposted	**Not signposted**
Interest rates are down again, this time by half of one per cent ...	Another half-per cent drop in interest rates ...
Floods have led to the evacuation of a thousand people from their homes in the West Country ...	A thousand people have been evacuated from their homes after flooding in the West Country ...
The world heavyweight champion, Mike Tyson ...	Mike Tyson, the world heavyweight champion ...

Signpost side-headings
Tonight's headlines ...
Now the economy ...
Next, the Middle East ...
Back home ...
So to tomorrow's weather ...
And the main points of the news again ...

Facts and figures
Stick to round numbers in your commentary and let the accompanying illustration take the strain.

Figures out this morning show the number of unemployed fell last month to just below two million

Europe's wine lake has grown again. Last year the wine-making countries produced nearly fifteen million more litres than they sold ...

Places
The same principle applies to places. It is easier to refer to general geographical locations and put the detail on accompanying maps.

The by-pass is being built to relieve traffic passing the historic school buildings on Harrow-on-the-Hill ...

The classic way: first the pictures, then the words.

Writing to Pictures

The test of a really good television script is whether it makes sense when heard with the eyes closed. Oddly, it shouldn't – quite – because what is missing is that essential pictorial dimension. So the starting point for any journalist who hopes to produce anything more than run-of-the-mill commentaries is recognition of the principle that words are tailored to pictures, not the other way round. It follows the only way this can be achieved is by viewing and assessing the edited material before writing the commentary.

Regrettably, time pressures on writers have become such that the temptation to take the lazy way out and dash off recorded commentaries to which the pictures are then cut to match has become almost irresistible. The result in most cases is dreary 'wallpaper' which adds nothing to understanding and almost certainly omits shots which would tell the story more effectively. Failing to give the picture editor freer rein to select the most appropriate pictures short-changes you, those who took the pictures, and the audience.

Golden rules of writing for television

- *View the pictures and listen to the sound.* While the picture editor's technical skills, advice and collaboration are essential ingredients, the journalist must be the arbiter when it comes to editorial priorities. It is impossible to judge the work you or others have done in the field unless you are present at the pre-edit stage.
- *Choose the pictures and sound most appropriate to the story you are aiming to tell.* Pay attention to any detail which might make a good script line and try to work out roughly what you might write. Don't be inhibited or hurried into agreeing to the inclusion of shots or sequences which are irrelevant, merely pretty, or do not contribute. If your story has been allocated a firm duration, work to it, otherwise you risk being asked to re-edit. At the same time, always be on the look-out for qualities which make your story of greater worth.
- *Leave the picture editor to edit.*
- *Shot-list the final version.* This is second in importance only to the Rule of Viewing. Shot-listing is a means of ensuring there will be an accurate match between words and pictures. The procedure consists of noting details of the length, picture and sound content of every scene in the edited story (see opposite.) As with the pictures-before-words principle, shot-listing may be regarded as old-fashioned, but be assured it will guarantee a better *product.*
- *Write the script working from the shot-list.*
- *Record the commentary.* If there is time, rehearse to make sure the words fit. If adjustment is needed, it is easier to change the script than the pictures.

Shot-listing example

Two very famous characters who are 'married' in a top-rated soap opera are also husband and wife in real life. They have just had their first child. A big crowd of fans waits to see them take baby Soapstar home from hospital, and the News assigns a reporter to provide a short scripted item marking the happy event.

At base, picture editor and reporter complete the first three stages of the six-stage editing and scripting process.

The picture editor sets the counter to zero on his cassette player. At the end of the first edit the machine is stopped so that the writer can put down on paper everything the scene contains, together with the clock time at the end of the first shot, say three seconds.

Close-up hospital entrance	3 sec

The machine is re-started and the pictures run on to the end of the next shot, which lasts four seconds. The reporter makes a note of the details and the cumulative time:

Zoom-out to general view of happy crowd in foreground	7 sec

The procedure is repeated until the end of the edited story, when the completed shot-list looks like this:

Close-up hospital entrance	3 sec
Zoom out to general view of happy crowd in foreground	7 sec
Mid-shot Mr and Mrs Soapstar appear with baby, smiling and waving as the crowd cheers	13 sec
Medium close-up Mrs Soapstar holding baby	17 sec
Long-shot smiling nurses wave from balcony	20 sec
Medium shot car arrives at hospital entrance	22 sec
Little girl is let through crowd to hand flowers to Mrs Soapstar	26 sec
Medium shot girl returns to place in the crowd	32 sec
Medium close-up Mrs Soapstar waves	37 sec
Medium shot Mr and Mrs Soapstar get into car	41 sec
Long-shot and pan, car drives off left to right	45 sec

Using the Shot-list

Try to start writing as soon as you have completed your shot-list, before the mental picture of your edited story begins to fade. Put three words – a second's worth of script – on each line of a ruled pad, or program your computer to do so. It is surprisingly easy to lose track once you have strung 30 or 40 seconds' worth of script across a page.

Do not waste time 'polishing' your prose as you go along. Complete as much of the script in rough as quickly as possible. First thoughts often turn out to be best, and in any case you may not have very much time for elegance.

It's not necessary always to start working out your commentary from the opening shot, especially if you are prone to writer's block. Select any *key scene* – in the case of our example, probably the moment, 22 seconds in, when the young fan hands her bouquet to Mrs Soapstar – and start to write around that. Once you are over the first hurdle, the rest of the script should begin to fall into place.

Common errors

● *Mistake One* is to try to cram in more words than the duration of the pictures will allow. Given the formula of three words a second, the 45 seconds of Mr and Mrs Soapstar's activities can be covered with a maxium of 135 words if they are still to make sense. More words than that and the pictures will actually run out. Let the pictures 'breathe'. The best script is often the one with the fewest words.

● *Mistake Two* is to write without taking proper notice of what the pictures contain. Instead there are detailed references to people, places or events which do not appear. It's guaranteed to irritate the viewer, who has come to expect to see whatever is being described. The same applies to sound. If it is necesary to refer to something which cannot be illustrated, do so obliquely without drawing attention to what may be missing from the coverage.

● *Mistake Three* is to produce what amounts to a series of captions explaining exactly what the audience is able to see for itself. Sentences will be too long and the style heavy, more suited to the printed page. Let the words and pictures 'touch', lightly and sensitively. Don't state the obvious or simply repeat what is happening on the screen, and vary the length of sentences to avoid sounding stilted.

● *Mistake Four* is carelessness about accuracy. Example: if you are writing about the number of cars on the road, the shot should show cars, not predominantly lorries or buses. If you are uncertain use general terms. In this case 'traffic' would cover anything from bicycles to juggernauts.

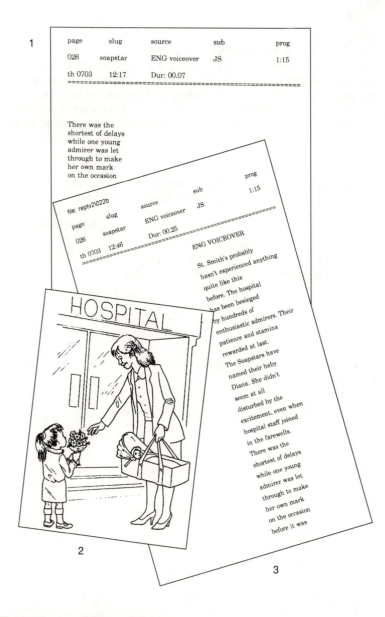

page	slug	source	sub	prog
026	soapstar	ENG voiceover	JS	1:15
th 0703	12:17	Dur: 00.07		

There was the
shortest of delays
while one young
admirer was let
through to make
her own mark
on the occasion

file: reptv21022b

			sub	prog
	slug	source	JS	1:15
page	soapstar	ENG voiceover		
026		Dur: 00.25		
th 0703	12:46			

ENG VOICEOVER

St. Smith's probably
hasn't experienced anything
quite like this
before. The hospital
has been besieged
by hundreds of
enthusiastic admirers. Their
patience and stamina
rewarded at last.
The Soapstars have
named their baby
Diana. She didn't
seem at all
disturbed by the
excitement, even when
hospital staff joined
in the farewells.
There was the
shortest of delays
while one young
admirer was let
through to make
her own mark
on the occasion
before it was

HOSPITAL

The mechanics of picture-scripting

Write one second's worth of script – three words – to each line. It's easier than stringing the commentary across the page when you are trying to match specific shots (1). It often helps to start by drafting your words around one key scene (2) rather than at the beginning of the pictures. The rest of the commentary should fall easily into place afterwards. If you are using a computer system it may do the job for you: in any case the final version (3) should be double-spaced and set out with the text on the right, the opposite side of the page left for technical and production instructions.

Sample script: Baby Soapstar goes home

A typical example of the scriptwriter's art: a routine, straightforward piece of work which has no special merit but follows all the rules. Two points to note in particular: (1) the words complement the pictures, neither competing with them nor describing what the audience can see for itself; (2) the length of the sentences varies, at times straddling more than on shot.

Presenter introduction:
The latest addition to the Soapstar family made her first public appearance this morning at the ripe old age of five days.

SHOT NO.	COMMENTARY	CUMULATIVE TIME
1. Close-up hospital entrance (setting the scene)	St Smith's probably hasn't known anything quite like this ...	0–1 sec 2 sec 3 sec
2. Zoom-out to general view of happy crowd in foreground (In reality the end of Shot 1)	... before. The hospital has been besieged by hundreds of enthusiastic fans. Their ...	4 sec 5 sec 6 sec 7 sec
3. Mid-shot Mr and Mrs Soapstar appear with baby, stand smiling and waving (No script)	... patience and stamina rewarded at last (CHEERS) (CHEERS) The Soapstars have named their baby ...	8 sec 9 sec 10 sec 11 sec 12 sec 13 sec
4. Medium close-up Mrs Soapstar holding baby (Not named until clearly in shot)	... Diana. She didn't seem at all disturbed by the excitement, even when ...	14 sec 15 sec 16 sec 17 sec
5. Long-shot nurses smile from balcony (Telescopes action to)	... hospital staff joined in the farewells. There was the ...	18 sec 19 sec 20 sec

Sample script (continued)

SHOT NO.	COMMENTARY	CUMULATIVE TIME
6. Medium shot car	... shortest of delays	21 sec
arrives at entrance	while one young	22 sec
as little girl is	admirer was let	23 sec
allowed through	through to make	24 sec
barrier to	her own mark	25 sec
present posy	on the occasion ...	26 sec
(The best moment)		
7. Medium shot girl	... before it was	27 sec
returns to her	time to go	28 sec
place in the crowd	home.	29 sec
(Commentary pause	(SOUND ONLY)	30 sec
for three	(SOUND ONLY)	31 sec
seconds)	(SOUND ONLY)	32 sec
8. Medium close shot	For Mrs Soapstar	33 sec
Mrs Soapstar waves	being a new	34 sec
(The moment to	mother makes no	35 sec
add more details	difference to her	36 sec
about her)	acting career. Next ...	37 sec
9. Medium shot Mr	... month she and	38 sec
and Mrs Soapstar get	Mr Soapstar start	39 sec
into car	rehearsals for a	40 sec
(Reference to him	new musical. So ...	41 sec
waits until they		
are both in shot)		
10. Long-shot and	... far there's no	42 sec
pan car drives off	part for Diana.	43 sec
(Script ends with	(SOUND ONLY)	44 sec
reference to baby	(SOUND ONLY)	45 sec
who is in the car, and		
there are two seconds		
leeway before the		
pictures run out)		

Fast, effective but strictly second-best.

Words before Pictures

Although the long-established pictures-before-words method of scripting described on pages 56–57 is considered difficult to beat for flexibility and sheer professional results every time, it is undoubtedly more time-consuming for both journalists and picture editors, and the pressures facing news people battling to overcome 'impossible' deadlines and/or the lack of facilities are such that any apparent short cut may be understandably seized upon and excused. Hence the popularity of an alternative process of compiling news items.

'Wild-track' commentary

In this method the complete commentary is written and recorded 'wild' on to a separate sound track *before* the pictures are edited. This can be done on location, in the studio or editing suite. No shot-listing is necessary. For very short routine items or segments of reports it can be fast and effective, but as a technique for lengthier or more considered pieces should be seen for what it is – strictly second-best and reserved for use only in emergencies. Unfortunately some reporters have never been introduced to the 'classic' way, while others are tempted to employ it as a blanket method for scripting all kinds of items, however unsuitable they may be.

Leave room for 'sound-bites'

If there is no alternative but to use this process, every effort should be made to view the raw material, either in the field or in the editing suite before a commentary is written and recorded. For in this context it is the words which govern the content and duration of the pictures being used. An imaginative script including a few sensible generalities should allow a competent picture editor to choose more widely from the available raw material. Too specific a script will force him or her to stick only to the obvious shots, resulting often in a duller outcome than the original coverage deserves. When recording the track remember to make room for any 'sound-bites', while pauses for natural sound effects will also help lift quality. Above all, take care to record in neutral surroundings, away from any extraneous, ambient sound which the editor would have difficulty masking when assembling the final version.

Influence of new technology

The influence on script-writing of future newsroom computer systems has yet to be fully assessed, though it does not seem likely that a journalist's ability to view raw or edited material on one side or through a 'window' on the screen of a desk-top editing terminal will necessarily encourage better writing standards.

In a multi-skilled world where few if any specialist picture editors exist the journalists will probably be compiling their own visual material. At least, if they have also shot it themselves they might have a better idea of the content. And that can only be good for the final product.

SEQUENCE	DURATION	CUMULATIVE	COMMENTARY
1	12 sec	12 sec	The planners say no-one could have possibly forecast the growth in traffic volume over the past few years. But they agree the time has now come to adopt a new approach to road-building.
2	21 sec	33 sec	Here in the grounds of a nine-hundred-year old estate less than two miles from one of Britain's busiest motorways, the roads of the future are being planned. The government has invested more than fifteen million pounds in a computer which will calculate future trends from current traffic flow. The hope is that traffic jams will become things of the past.
3	25 sec	58 sec	In the time of the Norman Conquest The Lodge belonged to a local baron who hunted boar across its extensive grounds. Probably the only sounds were those of laughter and merriment as the lords and ladies of the house feasted on chunks of roasted boar meat in the shade of the splendid oak which still dominates the front lawn. The irony isn't lost on John Smith, who's in charge of the project.
4	30 sec	1 min 28 sec	'One thing we simply have to get right ...'
5	20 sec	1 min 48 sec	Installation work on the computer is still continuing, and the project proper won't begin until test programs have been run. But there are signs that the experts will have no lack of information on which to base their future calculations. Traffic volume has already increased by almost one per cent in the few weeks since they have been here.
6	25 sec	2 min 13 sec	'I think we should have camera four moved to give a better view of that bridge, Brian. What do you think ...?'
7	10 sec	2 min 23 sec	But what guarantee is there that all the expense and effort going into this new project will result in forecasting which will be any more accurate than in the past?
8	30 sec	2 min 53 sec	'Well, of course there can be no guarantee. What I can say is ...'
9	17 sec	3 min 10 sec	On the evidence of the splendour in which he lived, it's not hard to feel envious of the Baron. Nor of his successors who strive for a sensible solution to a problem of society's own making. No-one will begrudge them their comfortable life-style if they find it.
10	30 sec	3 min 40 sec	The sceptical motorist down in these traffic jams is unlikely to be convinced, however much money is poured into projects like this one. No-one pretends traffic forecasting is easy: the price of oil, the drive towards a pollution-free atmosphere and the volatile Middle East all add to the uncertainty and have an influence on the number of cars on our roads. What I do believe is that hunting wild boar from the saddle couldn't have been much more tiring than driving home from the office along the crowded M180.

Words before pictures
A popular but second-best alternative technique for compiling television reports. A 'wild' commentary track is written and recorded and the pictures from the available raw material edited to match. Be sure to carry out the recording in a neutral environment or unwanted ambient sound may encroach on the sound track.

63

Your crew may be as 'green' as you are.

Introducing the News Camera

The special demands news makes of camera crews working alongside television reporters include the ability to think and work quickly, physical stamina, an understanding of editorial values and a willingness to accept an uncomplicated – one would say – simplistic – approach to their art.

They should also be conscious of being in constant local, regional, network or international competition. Crews and reporters are judged each day by results, by the pictures – or the story behind the pictures – they did or did not get.

Staff versus freelance
The big international news services employ their own staff camera teams to cover the world. Those denied such luxury may have to share with other sections of their organisation, suffering delay and uncertain quality if news has a low priority. Other permutations include the hiring of freelance crews contracted by the day or by the assignment and the creation of scratch teams made up of spare production or technical staff. So although at the highest level those who operate the camera are trained specialists, it does not always follow that your technical assistant knows much more than you do about the best way to tackle a story.

Camera crew numbers
In contrast to the numbers making up teams generally engaged on feature or documentary work, camera crews for news have historically stayed at a minimum. At most they consist of up to three people, not counting the reporter or a producer. Cost is an obvious factor in keeping down crew size, but far more important is the need for teams to be able to travel light and work quickly under pressure, perhaps in conditions where greater numbers would be a dangerous hindrance.

Single crewing
Within the past few years advances in camera technology and the introduction of more flexible working arrangements have led to the widespread application of single crewing. News teams now invariably consist of a camera operator who is responsible for all aspects of raw material gathering – pictures, sound and lighting – and a reporter. Two-person crews (camera and sound specialists) exist only where employer–union agreements decree so, and in war or other dangerous circumstances which demand the presence of a second member of the technical team for safety and morale.

Video journalists
The reduction in crew numbers to the ultimate minimum – journalist, camera operator, sound recordist and lighting assistant combined – has already taken place. Some local cable TV companies in particular have found this way of operating economical and effective in the expensive world of orthodox news-

The shrinking size of camera equipment

The 16 mm film camera was the versatile mainstay of television news programmes for more than twenty years in peace and war. Crews generally consisted of two people, one to operate the camera, the other the sound equipment. The magazine held a 400-foot roll of sound film, first mono then colour.

Electronic News Gathering. The 'Lightweight Revolution' of the mid-1970s introduced portable cameras with linked recorders using three-quarter-inch videotape housed in compact cassettes. Instant replay replaced film processing time, but in many news services camera teams continued to consist of two people.

Single Crewing. Compact, one-piece camcorders operated by a single person have added flexibility to news-gathering. The camera's built-in microphone and lights allow the operator to work without a reporter if necessary. The next step, combining the roles of journalist, camera, sound and lighting assistant, has already been taken by some organisations which see it as economical and effective.

gathering, training staff to shoot with lightweight cameras. The employers' argument is that the system enables them to hire and deploy more camera people and therefore broaden the agenda than the conventionalists are able to do. Despite the counter-argument that standards (that word again) inevitably suffer, there is no doubt the economic factor guarantees the practice will grow.

65

Camera Crew Who's Who

With the removal of the once-strict demarcation lines between crafts hastening the flexibility of working arrangements, it would be foolish to be dogmatic about the make-up of TV news camera crews, and it is no surprise to find two-person teams, single operators and video-journalists all jostling for position at the same news events. So in examining the main technical elements of news-gathering it is essential to be aware that some or all functions may be merged – with some practitioners also extending their range of skills to include picture editing, script writing or both.

Camera operators
Where two-person camera news teams remain in fashion, whoever operates the camera (US: photographer/videographer) is regarded as the senior member. Responsibility includes placing the camera in position, composing the picture and shooting the scene. Experienced camera-people are also respected for editorial nous gleaned over many assignments. Although as the reporter you are nominally in charge, if you are wise you will always listen to advice when it is offered.

Sound recordists
The recordist, where there is one, is chiefly responsible for ensuring speech levels are balanced and the right microphone is chosen for each assignment. Over the years the recordist's technical expertise has been extended to include first-line maintenance of the equipment. As a help towards promotion the recordist has traditionally been given opportunities to use the camera under supervision. The value of the recordist as chauffeur, 'fixer' and main trouble-shooter may also be seen on difficult or dangerous assignments.

Engineers
In some organisations sound recordists as a separate breed have been super-seded by versatile engineers whose multiplicity of duties includes general assistance to the camera operators but whose priority may be to ensure that the raw material, once gathered, is transmitted to base by the fastest possible route. This is usually by the microwave links or satellite systems which have become commonplace in news-gathering, especially abroad.

Electricians
Lighting assistants – electricians or 'sparks' – tend to operate independently of the rest of the team. Their equipment probably consists of a portable rig of hand-held and free-standing lights powerful enough to provide the supplementary illumination by which film or videotape can be shot at indoor or poorly lit locations. News-camera teams are equipped with their own basic set of lights, good enough for most routine events, in addition to the light fitment available for attaching to the camera itself. As each new generation of lenses becomes more versatile and light-sensitive than the last, the number of occasions when separate lighting for news coverage is needed is fast being reduced.

The camera team
Advances in technology and the decline in strict demarcation between crafts has brought a flexible approach to news-gathering. The functions illustrated may be merged or extended.

Camera
Operator composes picture, records scene. In news, increasingly likely to work solo with one-piece camcorder equipped with built-in microphone and light.

Recordist/engineer
Responsible for microphone choice, first-line equipment maintenance, and seeing raw material from the camera is transmitted by the fastest possible route. Camera-operator's 'eyes and ears' on dangerous assignments.

Electrician
A disappearing breed for routine news-gathering as camera teams may be equipped with their own set of portable lights.

67

... take advice from an experienced camera operator.

Part of the Team

Until the all-purpose video-journalist becomes the norm, news-gathering in television will continue to be the work of at least two people – the camera operator and you the reporter. For most practitioners the idea of specialist support is an attractive one, as the involvement of a separate camera operator allows the reporter to concentrate entirely on editorial matters.

Yet it is a curiosity of television journalism that it concentrates such power in the hands of a non-journalist: whatever motives are ascribed to and criticisms made of reporters, strangely little attention is paid to camera people, who make editorial decisions every time they point the lens towards one scene in preference to another. This is in complete contrast to radio or print journalism, where the technicians have a wholly non-editorial role and where their assistance does not come into the reckoning until the reporter's work is finished.

So it is arguable whether a television report can ever be any better than the camera will allow. Certainly the role is a crucial one and the early stages of your career can in large measure be made or marred by the temperament and ability of those assigned to operate the camera: you can learn a lot about your own job from the way your camera-toting colleagues go about theirs.

Discuss content

Try to strike up a good relationship right from the start. Get into the habit of discussing the proposed shape and content of your item before you begin work and, particularly when you are inexperienced, be guided by the advice and ideas of others. Be trusting. Although as a young reporter you may be extremely apprehensive about the 'technical side', you will rarely be let down: professional pride ensures professional camera-people recognise that if the reporter fails, so do they. Nevertheless, however green you are, you may always be expected to take the lead on location, so the relationship can be a difficult one. At times it may be necessary to insist on following through your own ideas against what may seem to be better judgement. If and when you are proved wrong be big enough to admit it.

Sensitivities

It is equally important not to overlook the professional sensitivities of others. For example, never attempt to 'play the director'. It is time-consuming and can seem pretentious, as television journalism does not go in for feature-film technique. Wait to be invited to look through the viewfinder when a shot is being composed. If it happens it is a privilege not to be taken for granted.

Finally, remember that the camera operator's responsibility for pictorial content includes an awareness of the need to shoot pictures with deadlines and the editing process in mind, so in hard news situations do not expect other than sharp, unfussy camera-work.

The importance of camera-people
The television reporter is part of a team, so make full use of the experience of others working with you. Camera-people who take a pride in their work are happy to pass on their expertise to young reporters, and will do their best to ensure a successful end-product. But they don't respect arrogance or over-confidence.

Camera and Sound Equipment

The development of camera equipment has come a long way since the days when the newsreels went to war with the 35 mm gear similar to that used in the making of feature films. First there was a switch to the lighter, more mobile 16 mm – originally derided an amateur format – complete with magnetic sound track, fast chemical processing and updated editing techniques. Twenty years later, by the end of the 1970s, had come a further revolution which saw film virtually swept away altogether in favour of re-usable, instantly replayable videotape. The after-shocks of that upheaval are still being felt as developments in digital technology spearhead the drive towards more compact, one-piece digital video cameras (DVC) using tapes the size of matchboxes or even disks to record material.

Electronic news gathering
The commonly accepted term for the lightweight video equipment used in news is Electronic News Gathering (ENG), although other terminology, including Electronic Journalism (EJ), and Portable Single Camera (PSC) also exists.

The first widely used ENG equipment consisted of a camera weighing a few pounds/kilos and a separate, portable videocassette machine on which both picture and sound were recorded on to three-quarter-inch (19 mm) tape. This was followed first by Betacam, a half-inch (12.5 mm) tape system introduced by Sony, the Japanese company, then by Betacam SP (Superior Performance), a format which became the industry standard.

Enter the camcorder
The incorporation of the recorder *within* the camera body itself was the next logical development. It had other important implications, too, for it made the separate sound recordist redundant, as one person could now operate the equipment by him- or herself, using the camera-mounted microphone to capture the sound. Where necessary extra microphones could be plugged in and handled by the reporter. For news, this principle of 'single-crewing', with the users employing any one of a broadening range of professional standard camcorders, has become widely adopted, offering the additional prospect of the complete 'one-man/woman band' – camera-operator and journalist all rolled into one.

The advantage of ENG
The main advantage for news work is its mobility and speed, as there is no wasteful processing time. It is also extremely versatile in other ways. The raw material can be extracted and handed over for despatch and editing; the signals can be transmitted direct to base or by an intermediate microwave link; they can be transmitted live and recorded at the same time. Tape in particular is cheap and re-useable, and the pictures and sound can be transferred by playing them from cassette to cassette or cassette to non-linear editor. Material edited electronically is never actually 'cut', the original remaining intact.

Editing

TRANSMISSION

Advantages of ENG
One-piece camcorder offers speed and flexibility. Sound and pictures can be recorded onto tape or disk for delivery by hand or transmitted over microwave link direct to home base, or to an intermediate point. 'Live' transmission facilities are also possible, if necessary via satellite.

Don't let the stick mic wave about.

Sound

One-piece camcorders come equipped with a microphone clipped to the top of the camera body. It picks up sound from the direction in which the camera is pointed. On some models the microphone can be removed from its cradle and hand-held by the reporter or another member of the team. Other ENG systems have leads plugged into the cassette recorder, allowing a variety of micro-phones to be attached according to location and conditions. Four main types are in use for news.

Personal microphone
This is light, inconspicuous and particularly favoured for use by reporters and subjects in interviews. It comes in at least two versions – one is attached to a cord which slips over the head, while another (also known as a lapel micro-phone) clips directly onto clothing. Both rest at about chest height, so helping to keep out background noise. In either case the connecting lead, which looks untidy if seen in shot, can be easily hidden from view.

Directional microphone
Sometimes known as the rifle or gun mike, it is aimed at the speaker by the recordist. Its long, thin barrel is usually covered by a metal baffle as protection against wind noise. This microphone picks up sound through a narrow angle over long distances. Its drawback is its unfortunate weapon-like shape – highly dangerous in some circumstances – and the tendency for handlers to let it creep into shot.

Stick microphone
This is the simplest in the recordist's bag. It is extremely popular for use by reporters doing stand-up pieces. Very little preparation is required, and it is adaptable for most purposes. Grasp it firmly near the head. If you are using it during an interview it should be 'favoured' gently towards the speaker and not thrust forwards aggressively.

Radio microphone
With the advantage of allowing you freedom from any cable attachment to the camera equipment, the radio mike consists of a personal-type microphone and a miniature transmitter which slips into the pocket. The device enables your voice to carry over several hundred yards/metres and, used sparingly, can be very effective.

Other microphone types
These are more likely to be used in studios than on location. Stand mikes offer high-quality sound at the expense of obtrusiveness, and boom mikes (direc-tional microphones controlled by boom operators) can create annoying shadows.

72

Microphone types
Personal microphones come in two types, one with a cord which slips over the head
(1), and another which clips on to clothing (2). Directional microphones (3) have a
weapon-like appearance. The stick microphone (4) is versatile and soon ready for use,
while the radio mike (5) comes in two parts – a personal microphone and a miniature
transmitter.

Master this technique above all.

Stand-uppers

The stand-upper (stand-up or piece to camera) has always been considered one of the mainstay techniques of television reporting, although it goes in and out of favour according to fashion. It remains a yardstick against which confidence in front of the camera is measured, and while there is nothing complicated about the technique, no reporter is likely to make serious career progress without mastering it.

The term speaks for itself. The stand-upper consists of a straightforward spoken delivery to the camera – and through it to the audience. Also:

- It establishes the reporter's presence on the spot.
- It takes little time to do.
- It offers versatility because it can be used by itself or as a single ingredient within a story.

Given a choice, some reporters prefer not to use the stand-upper at all, believing they have failed if they have to resort to their own talking head instead of what they consider should be more adequate illustration. Others are reticent because, surprisingly, they lack the technique, which depends on three things:

- An ability to compose direct, spoken language.
- A good memory.
- Fluent, confident delivery.

The emphasis on good, broadcast-style writing has already been stressed, so let us examine the other main requirements.

The right backgrounds
These are essential to all stand-uppers, which are intended to prove to the viewer that reporters are where they say they are. Pieces to camera are enhanced by relevant backgrounds, which should always be preferred to those offering only anonymity. It's worth taking time to investigate the most appropriate setting, but be sure to consult your camera crew before deciding where to place yourself. Don't allow so much to go on in the background that the viewer will not be interested in what you have to say. Noisy settings can be just as distracting. And never leave the audience wondering why a particular background has been chosen. Opening words must be sure to set the scene.

Centre-screen or to one side?
Some news organisations like their reporters to be positioned in the centre of the picture while delivering stand-uppers. They believe it adds authority. Others with an eye on the composition prefer the performer to stand to one side or the other, arguing that in this way the reporter becomes part of the scene and does not appear to be a superimposition on it. You may not be given the choice. If you are, err on the side of consistency.

1

2

3

4

5

Stand-uppers

Find an appropriate place from which to tell your story. A background will put your piece in context (1), but take care not to distract the audience by cluttering the screen with too much detail (2). An anonymous setting is boring and adds nothing (3). Some news organisations prefer their reporters to be positioned centre-screen (4). Others believe picture composition is enhanced by placing the reporter to one side.

Memory Aids

The most obvious problem you face in preparing your first stand-upper is remembering the words. For those whose nerves let them down to the extent that they are unable to memorise anything, ad-libbing is not the answer. It rarely comes across as convincing, especially if it is not fluent, and in circumstances where strict accuracy of thought and language are necessary, it can be very risky.

How to remember the words
For the beginner, the secret is to proceed cautiously and not to be over-ambitious. First, write down what you are going to say and memorise it. If you can remember a five-line limerick you can manage 30 words – the equivalent of ten seconds. When that seems easy, increase it in 15-word – five-second – stages until you have reached a comfortable, sensible limit.

Alternatives
If circumstances demand that your piece lasts for 40 seconds, and the best you can manage is 20 seconds, do not try to speak your lines in one continuous take. Seek the co-operation of the camera crew in learning and recording your words in two separate chunks. Make sure you are framed sufficiently differently in each half so the result will not look odd when the two takes are edited together. It is ugly but effective.

Another way out is to ensure that at least the opening and closing paragraphs are word-perfect, and to read the rest from a notebook or clipboard. Make sure this is in shot, or viewers will be left wondering what you are looking at.

Electronic prompting
Technology is on hand if none of these methods works. Field versions exist of the electronic prompting devices normally used in studio work (see page 119), though these tend to be reserved for scripts associated with lengthy documentaries rather than straight news.

Miniature tape recorders
A second, increasingly used aid comes in the shape of the tiny, battery-operated cassette machines used as audio-notebooks or as players of pre-recorded music tapes. First, the stand-upper script is written and recorded. The recorder is then kept out of shot while the reporter performs for the camera, listening to the replayed tape through the earpiece and repeating the words aloud. With practice this is the most effective method of improving fluency of delivery, although it is obviously important to be able to keep a sentence or so ahead of the recording and to concentrate on speaking as well as listening. The earpiece must fit snugly enough not to give the game away. And don't forget to change the recorder batteries.

Aid to memory

If you lack confidence in your ability to remember lines, a miniature tape-recorder with attached earpiece (1) will make you appear fluent under almost all circumstances. Once you have written the script (2) and recorded it, put the machine in your pocket. The earpiece is visible from the side as you speak, prompted by the replayed tape (3). Take proper care, and the camera – and the audience – sees only a confident performance (4) (Author). A less sophisticated aid is the 'idiot board' which, at its crudest, consists of a handwritten script held below or to one side of the camera.

1

2

3

4

The Art of Interviewing

Interviewing is an art which is approached with far less careful thought than it deserves. There is more to it than the routine, all-purpose line of questioning which scarcely varies whatever the topic – the journalistic equivalent of the telephone sales pitch. The best interviewers are not satisfied unless every time they appear they unearth a small nugget of truth or open the door to wider understanding. Beginners have a tendency to think of all television interviews in the terms of the lengthy, combative setpieces conducted in studios at prime time and are surprised to discover the existence of a wide range of types, each calling for subtle differences in approach.

Preparation
The first rule of interviewing has nothing to do with journalistic ethics or technique. It is: find out who you are interviewing and why. Don't wait until the camera is rolling and expect the interviewee to come to your rescue. Some will. Others will enjoy your discomfort and the opportunity it presents. Nothing is more guaranteed to undermine your credibility with the audience and dent your confidence than an interview which gets off on the wrong foot, the subject prefacing the answer to your first question with the correction to a name or title. Embarrassment all round – at your expense.

Once you are armed with the basic details, ask yourself what you expect from the interview. Facts for the record? An opinion? Or a mixture of both? Is it to be short and incisive or leisurely and gently probing?

The extent and depth of your research will, of course, vary according to the kind of interview involved and the time allotted to it. A thorough examination of background material is more likely to be necessary for a searching political interview than with the eye-witness to a robbery.

Questions
Some journalists do not prepare questions in advance, preferring to 'wing it' and let the interview run its natural course. There are very few circumstances in which this is a good idea, and few practitioners can get away with the technique. Spraying questions about as they come to mind is undisciplined and is bound to lead to confusion, omission and repetition. Aim to approach the subject naturally and logically.

But unless there is a danger of running out of questions there is no need to write down a long list and stick to it regardless. If you are afraid of 'drying' it is worth jotting down a few to jog the memory. Spontaneity is better achieved with a broad outline of the ground to be covered and the details left until the interview gets under way.

The set-piece interview (1)
One of the main categories to be found either in the studio or on location, the classic single-camera set-up has the lens pointing over your shoulder at the interview subject.

Detailed rehearsal ruins spontaneity.

Interview Preparation

Most interviews benefit from spontaneity, so it is not a good idea to go over questions in detail. For the same reason avoid 'dry runs' or rehearsals with or without the camera, which risk nervous or inexperienced interviewees 'talking themselves out' before the real thing begins. But as the purpose of any interview is to extract something of value for the audience, the subject should be given a general idea of the ground to be covered and the shape the interview is intended to take.

Submitting questions
Do not readily agree to submit questions in advance unless it is the only way of securing an important or much sought-after interview, and – apart from rare and unusual circumstances – do not concede the right of veto over part or all of the finished product.

Judge on its merits a condition that an interviewee will agree to an appearance on the strict understanding that a particular subject will not be covered or a particular question not asked. It depends on how badly you want the interview. Quite often, as a well-conducted interview proceeds, it becomes possible to raise the contentious issue after all. On other occasions, if it would appear ridiculous not to ask the burning question of the hour, a refusal to answer – and the manner of that refusal – may be worthwhile in its own right. But once you have accepted conditions, stick to your word. Anything else would be unethical.

Tone
Much of the criticism made of interviewers is to do with their 'tone'. Accept that you will rarely be judged as having got it exactly right. Viewers' opinions are inevitably coloured by their own prejudices and perceptions, and it is not unusual for one half of the audience to believe, quite genuinely, that you have been too hard and aggressive and the other half – just as genuinely – that you have been too soft and tentative.

Faced with this conundrum every day, try to forget how the audience might react and seek to adopt a tone which suits the occasion. Sometimes it is necessary to pursue an interviewee who appears to be trying to avoid giving answers to legitimate questions. Regrettably that has become a tactic commonly employed by politicians and others. But there are basic courtesies to be observed, and remember that interviewees have the ultimate sanction: they can always walk away if they do not like the way they are being treated.

Set-piece interviews (2)
The set-piece is usually shot in medium close-up, concentrating on the interviewee (1). Rather than stop the camera, ensure any running changes to composition are carried out during your questions (2) which can then be edited out (3).

Rule: ask questions, don't make statements.

Interview Technique

The technique of interviewing for television is very different from that used by journalists who work in the medium of print. Newspaper journalists are able to conduct their interviews over the telephone or in some quiet corner accompanied by nothing more technical than a drink, pencil and notebook or miniature tape-recorder. The occasion can be formal or informal to suit, with questions asked and clarification sought in any manner which seems appropriate. Questions and answers do not have to be grammatical or follow a logical path, for once back at the keyboard the journalist can tidy up the product and make it fit any desired shape.

The television reporter's work is nothing if not public. At the very least the interview is conducted in the presence of one technician with the camera, which immediately creates an air of artificiality. And then the interviewer's technique is subjected to a scrutiny to which the newspaper journalist is never put.

Putting the questions
There is always an element of 'performance' in every interview. Be conscious of it, even though your questions may be edited out.
- Don't gabble.
- Be clear and unambiguous.
- Ask questions, do not make statements which leave the interviewee wondering whether to answer.
- Keep questions short, but not so short that they scarcely register.
- Remember that the audience is more interested in the interviewee's answers than your questions.
- Once you have asked a question, let the interviewee answer. If you have to interrupt, do so when there is a natural pause. Recordings of overlapping voices are impossible to edit.
- If an interview strays too far off the subject, bring it back on course. If necessary, stop the camera, explain to the interviewee what is going wrong, and start again.
- Avoid 'warm-up' questions. They waste time.
- Do not preface every question with deferential words or phrases which suggest timidity. Typical examples: 'May I/Could I/Do you mind if I ask ...?'
- Be bold and direct – but being too brusque will be counterproductive.
- Take care not to ask questions which invite one-word answers, usually 'Yes' or 'No'. Rephrase.

Supplementaries
Some novice interviewers concentrate so much on asking their questions that they forget to listen to the answers. Always be prepared to ask supplementaries, and if the interview suddenly takes off in an unexpected, more interesting direction, follow.

1   2

3

Interview technique
Position the subject slightly to one side, looking towards the empty side of the screen (1). 'Profile' shot has the interviewee looking out of screen and seeming to exclude the audience (2). The camera operator's view should be two to three inches (50–75 mm) above the subject's eyeline (3).

Cliché questions
Some questions are asked so frequently they have become clichés. Avoid especially:
- How do you feel (about) …?
- What of the future?
- What's your reaction to …?
- Just how serious …?
- Just what …?
- Just when …?
- Just why …?

These are just irritating.

Interview Types

Most interviews fall into one of a limited number of categories. At this stage it is important to differentiate, so what we are examining here are those conducted out on location with an ENG team. Interview types which take place in front of the studio cameras are discussed on pages 124–140.

Set-piece interviews

Set-pieces provide much of the bread-and-butter material for inclusion in reporter packages pages 88–91. They presuppose the interviewee's willingness to participate, which means that on occasions arrangements can be made far enough in advance for the reporter to undertake some proper preparation.

This form of interview is likely to take place on the interviewee's own ground, and will tend to be used to gather opinion and interpretation rather than fact.

A typical set-piece for news-related programmes probably consists of no more than six or seven questions. Make sure the interview follows a logical pattern with a recognisable beginning, middle and end, so that afterwards it is possible to select a coherent chunk rather than edit fiercely. Less time will be spent in the cutting room and what appears on the screen won't seem 'bitty'.

Put the interview in context by setting it against a relevant background. If there's a sensible alternative to the anonymous office, use it. During the interview the camera will probably point over your shoulder at the interviewee, framed in medium close-up, and only your voice will be heard. Any necessary changes of shot and angle should take place only during the questions, which are likely to be edited out of the final version and replaced with 'cutaways' (see page 86).

Doorstepping

The term 'doorstep interview' is more or less self-explanatory. The reporter waits – sometimes literally on the doorstep of a building – for an interviewee to appear. A special target may be in mind, or it could be that anyone who is willing to talk will be pounced on and interviewed.

Questions are usually straightforward – typically connected with the outcome of official meetings or negotiations.

Doorstepping tends to be a fairly hit-or-miss method of interviewing. It is not much liked by reporters, although some useful material is often forthcoming. It is also surprising how regularly what begins as a shouted question from a few yards away ends with the person who has been 'doorstepped' agreeing to take part in a proper interview.

Doorsteppers, by their nature, demand a large measure of patience, stamina, and willingness to push through the rest of the media crowd to point a microphone at the right person.

In the melee, don't forget to take the camera crew with you.

Don't go blundering in with insensitive questions.

Eyewitnesses and Others

Eye-witness or spot interviews seek mostly factual information, so this is where the old-fashioned journalistic ability to persuade someone to talk to the camera comes to the fore. Eye-witnesses to accidents, other disasters, and crime, provide the stuff of hard-news reporting, and such interviews are probably the easiest to conduct. There is no mystique to the technique, but do not go blundering in with questions which are insensitive or intrusive.

Vox pops
The generally accepted accuracy of opinion polls has tended to make the use of vox pops (vox populi) in television news programmes appear out-dated. They were probably never intended as anything more than a cross-section of views taken at random, but they had the merit of providing a few ordinary members of the public with a chance to give their opinion. If used at all, vox pops are more likely now to be sought on humorous subjects.

The technique relies on exactly the same question being asked of each interviewee so that answers can be edited together without the reporter popping up in between.

One point to do with picture composition: try to have each interviewee framed in the same way – medium to close-up. 'Jump' cut effects are avoided by asking contributors to look alternately camera right and camera left.

News conferences
News conferences are group interviews, held as alternatives to separate sessions, with perhaps hundreds of journalists. They usually begin with state-ments by one or any number of people, followed by an open question and answer session. Unless there is a prearranged order, the problem for television reporters is how to put their question when others are trying to do the same, and at times when the camera may not be in a position to roll. To make matters worse, if there is more than one interviewee, as often happens, there is no guarantee the question will be answered by the person at whom it is directed.

As an information-gathering exercise the news conference may be accept-able, but generally it is another form of 'interview' not much liked by reporters. It smacks of news-management, because if several journalists are asking questions at once, 'the platform' is likely to choose not to hear the most awkward ones. The ideal solution is to shoot some scene-setting material and seek separate interviews afterwards. If this proves impossible, take your chances along with everyone else. Make sure your recordist positions the microphone on the 'top table', preferably fixing it firmly to the public address mike. In that way you are sure of picking up all the answers clearly, and if necessary voice-over questions can be added later.

Don't cheat in your cutaway questions.

Cutaway Questions

Reporter cutaway questions (inserts or reverses) are recorded in case the picture editor needs to bridge chosen sections of an interview shot on a single camera. It is a cinematic editing device, the intention being to avoid the ugly, on-screen 'jump cut'.

For the reporter, the technique relies on an ability to repeat the original questions for the camera as naturally as in the interview, even though the interviewee is probably no longer with you. Consult your original list or replay the interview to ensure keeping to the questions as closely as possible. Some sticklers for accuracy record their interviews on personal cassette-machines and play them back before asking the cutaways. While it is probably just about acceptable to tidy up the occasional grammatical error, be careful not to cheat by putting an entirely different construction on a question.

Noddies
Serving the same purpose as the cutaway is the 'noddy' – a shot of the reporter nodding in response to the interviewee's answer. This device should be used sparingly, as a 'noddy' could give a misleading impression that you agree with what is being said. Some news organisations ban 'noddies' and cutaway questions altogether, in the belief that the viewer has a right to be aware that editing has taken place.

Both devices depend on a correct positioning of the camera. If it is wrong, the edited version will give the impression that interviewer and interviewee are looking in the same direction, not at each other.

Interview editing
In countries where a degree of press freedom exists, it is understood that television interviews are subject to editing, those for news and news-related programmes most of all.

Yet the whole subject remains an area of controversy, an ever-present source of potential conflict – not so much with those in the public eye, but with those who are unfamiliar with journalistic practice. The complaint is then usually of 'misrepresentation' or 'distortion'. Regrettably there is often no answer which will satisfy the complainant, although it should be possible to prove that you have acted fairly and in good faith.

The main thing is never to give an undertaking to include or exclude a particular answer or passage. Whatever your own good intentions, it might be impossible to keep your promise, as the decision about editing may rest with someone more senior. In all cases, before you start to interview an inexperienced person it is advisable to make it clear that you are under no obligation to use all or any of what is said.

Cutaway questions
When a single camera is used it concentrates on the interviewee (1). Shots of the reporter are taken afterwards to act as a bridge between edited sections, thus avoiding ugly 'jump-cuts on the screen'. (2) Unless care is taken in setting up these 'cutaway questions' both interviewee and interviewer will seem to be looking in the same direction, not at each other. The technique is beginning to fall out of favour for news-type programmes.

87

Constructing a Package (1)

The biggest test of all-round journalistic ability comes with the creation of 'packages' combining the basic reporting skills with an understanding of television production techniques.

Packages have no set shape or duration, but as the reporter's way of story-telling they must follow a clear, logical thread and sustain interest, whatever the subject.

Occasionally, especially at first, you may have an editorial help-mate to guide you through the intricacies. Mostly, you are on your own. In the past, an experienced camera team could always be counted on to make an important contribution, but with the scaling down of camera units to a size where you might be expected to operate some of the equipment as well, knowledge of production methods is an essential ingredient of your professional education.

For the purpose of this exercise, assume that the team consists of three – reporter, camera operator and recordist.

Research
As we have already seen, some research, however limited, is a prerequisite for all good television reporting. It does not have to be sophisticated, consisting at its most basic only of ensuring that you and the crew are together in the right place at the right time.

Then it is important to know what the story is about. The treatment and degree of difficulty involved clearly vary according to the subject. With proper planning, including a reasonable amount of preparation time, some information can be established before you set out; background material if it exists, names of potential interviewees on or off camera.

Planning the shape
Unless they are straightforward 'hard news' stories calling for an intuitive approach on the spot, most news packages fall within a predictable framework. Variety comes from the order, number and duration of each ingredient, so the overall shape of a package can be considered and a provisional treatment planned without prejudging editorial value.

The 'recce'
Where possible take the opportunity to conduct research on the spot. While a full-scale 'recce' is a bonus – in documentary-type work it ought to be manda-tory – simple matters settled in advance will add to the speed and efficiency of the camera operation when it takes place. Journalists are indeed required to be flexible in their approach, but if 'making it up as you go along' can be avoided, so much the better.

At worst, aim to arrive on the scene a few minutes before the camera team to spy out the land, make contact with contributors, decide the location of the main interviews and note requirements for supporting shots.

Current theory suggests that longer, thoroughly researched packages may also lend themselves to pre-scripting.

Whatever the subject, the typical reporter package should be so well-constructed that the audience is unaware of the joins. Voice-over commentary should dovetail neatly into and out of interview extract; the stand-upper should pick up smoothly, verbally, visually and acoustically – a tribute to the hard work, thought and professionalism which has gone into the construction of the item.

Knowing what to shoot

Camera crews rarely turn up at the scene of a news story, leap from their cars and record everything in sight. Most news gathering is better-ordered and more organised than that. It is as bad to have too much coverage as it is too little. Someone eventually has to view it, and having to plough through an hour's video rushes to select the relevant rushes for a three-minute report is unhelpful and unnecessary. The cheapness and reusability of videotape is a constant invitation to over-shooting, but this should be resisted. Raw newsfilm in its heyday in the 1960s and early 1970s came in 400-foot rolls of 16 mm, and there was much discussion about the ratio of footage shot to footage transmitted, and the cost involved.

Editorial partnership

By now it should be clear that a well-constructed report is the product of a satisfactory working relationship between reporter and camera crew. But it is necessary to be aware of the limitations of equipment and the time it takes to arrange complicated camera set-ups. Understand that technical difficulties can disrupt the best-laid plans.

Usually, with experienced and co-operative camera crews, it is enough to give a general outline of what you want, but don't hesitate to act positively and direct the work to ensure that your ideas are followed through.

Accompany the crew

Every reporter should make a habit of accompanying the camera crew as they go about their business to make detailed notes about each shot or sequence. In circumstances where this is not possible, brief your colleagues as fully as possible.

The aim is to ensure that voice-over commentary makes fullest use of the available pictures, and this cannot be achieved without knowing exactly what they contain. With the right video equipment it is possible to view recorded material on site, but writing blind to other people's descriptions invariably leads to bland and unimaginative scripts.

Constructing a Package (2)

An understanding of the rudiments of film direction is a valuable asset to any reporter. This has not always been the case. When news items were short and uncomplicated it was scarcely necessary. But now that some reports qualify almost as miniature documentaries, the need has been created for better technique. Formal training is increasing, though not necessarily fast enough, and those still waiting should aim to learn all they can working alongside their colleagues in the camera crew.

The grammar of pictures
Despite the general simplicity of its approach, news filming tries to conform to accepted pictorial grammar. Audience understanding of technique has been stretched over the years by what has appeared on the big and small screen, but the conventions should not be broken unless they further enhance understanding.

In particular, do not expect to tell your story effectively through an assemblage of single, unrelated shots. Always think in sequences leading the viewer progressively towards the action: long-shot, mid-shot, close-shot.

Picture composition
Few professional camera crews will like it if you insist on looking through the viewfinder before every shot. But that should not stop your journalistic eye being kept open for good backgrounds which help tell the story, or for errors in picture composition which might have been overlooked in the haste of news gathering. Try not to let interviewees appear to sprout trees, lamp-posts or other objects from their head as they speak. Look out for spectators creeping into shot or other background goings-on while the crew are absorbed in their work.

Be aware of what is written on walls over interviewees' shoulders or behind you during a stand-upper. It could be seriously offensive or inappropriate. Don't be tempted to take risks because it's in a foreign language. Someone will understand it, even if you don't. The same goes for street signs and advertisements which could distract the viewer during your report. The safe rule is: if in doubt – find another wall.

Sound
Television is two-dimensional. With the picture goes the sound. 'Natural' sound – 'effects' in this context – is often under-used by reporters who scarcely pause for breath, preferring to fill every available second with their own voice or those of interviewees.

Listen for any opportunity to make use of the natural sounds of life. They will give your work an extra quality. Some stories are simply better told by limiting the talk and letting the sound speak for itself.

1

2

3

4

Basic camera shots
Think in picture sequences, not unrelated single shots. Long shot (1) shows the whole of a human figure; medium shot (2) shows from the waist up; medium close-up (3) shows from the chest up; close-up (4) shows head and shoulders.

Package example

STORY: the installation of a new computer system aimed at easing traffic flow in a particularly busy part of Britain.

WORKING TITLE: COMPUTER TRAFFIC.

PROPOSED DURATION: 3 min 30 sec.

OUTLINE TREATMENT: find out the reason for the project, see those at work on it and ask for their opinion of its value; contrast the beauty and tranquillity of the surroundings with the subject – traffic noise and congestion.

INGREDIENTS: shots of traffic (recent archive material if necessary); computer being installed; monitoring equipment; building and grounds; interviews with project leader; piece to camera; electronic graphics; voice-over commentary.

INTRODUCTION: by Presenter in studio, with map to show location.

ORDER OF CONTENTS:

1. Voice-over commentary to accompany recent archive pictures of traffic congestion in area (planned duration 15 sec).
2. Piece-to-camera (stand-upper) in grounds explaining how a former stately home has become a centre for the planning of road-building and traffic control (planned duration 20 sec).
3. Voice-over commentary to cover exteriors of building (planned duration 25 sec).
4. Interview (one answer) with project leader (planned duration 30 sec).
5. Voice-over commentary to show other staff at work collating information (planned duration 20 sec).
6. Natural sound as computer operators monitor traffic flow on video screens (planned duration 25 sec).
7. Voice-over commentary showing reverse angle of computer operation (planned duration 10 sec).
8. Second part of interview with project leader (planning duration 30 sec).
9. Summarising voice-over commentary showing restored part of building (planned duration 15 sec).
10. Final piece-to-camera on bridge overlooking traffic (planned duration 25 sec).

SEQUENCE	DURATION	CUMULATIVE	COMMENTARY
1	12 sec	12 sec	The planners say no-one could have possibly forecast the growth in traffic volume over the past few years. But they agree the time has now come to adopt a new approach to road-building.
2	21 sec	33 sec	Here in the grounds of a nine-hundred-year old estate less than two miles from one of Britain's busiest motorways, the roads of the future are being planned. The government has invested more than fifteen million pounds in a computer which will calculate future trends from current traffic flow. The hope is that traffic jams will become things of the past.
3	25 sec	58 sec	In the time of the Norman Conquest The Lodge belonged to a local baron who hunted boar across its extensive grounds. Probably the only sounds were those of laughter and merriment as the lords and ladies of the house feasted on chunks of roasted boar meat in the shade of the splendid oak which still dominates the front lawn. The irony isn't lost on John Smith, who's in charge of the project.
4	30 sec	1 min 28 sec	'One thing we simply have to get right ...'
5	20 sec	1 min 48 sec	Installation work on the computer is still continuing, and the project proper won't begin until test programs have been run. But there are signs that the experts will have no lack of information on which to base their future calculations. Traffic volume has already increased by almost one per cent in the few weeks since they have been here.
6	25 sec	2 min 13 sec	'I think we should have camera four moved to give a better view of that bridge, Brian. What do you think ...?'
7	10 sec	2 min 23 sec	But what guarantee is there that all the expense and effort going into this new project will result in forecasting which will be any more accurate than in the past?
8	30 sec	2 min 53 sec	'Well, of course there can be no guarantee. What I can say is ...'
9	17 sec	3 min 10 sec	On the evidence of the splendour in which he lived, it's not hard to feel envious of the Baron. Nor of his successors who strive for a sensible solution to a problem of society's own making. No-one will begrudge them their comfortable life-style if they find it.
10	30 sec	3 min 40 sec	The sceptical motorist down in these traffic jams is unlikely to be convinced, however much money is poured into projects like this one. No-one pretends traffic forecasting is easy: the price of oil, the drive towards a pollution-free atmosphere and the volatile Middle East all add to the uncertainty and have an influence on the number of cars on our road. What I do believe is that hunting wild boar from the saddle couldn't have been much more tiring than driving home from the office along the crowded M180.

What to Keep In, What to Leave Out

A new reporter faced for the first time with extracting anything between one minute and four minutes of newsworthy material from a pile of raw rushes will find it a daunting task. What to keep in? What to take out? This is part of the reporter's authorship – no two reporters might construct the story in the same way. In some newsrooms the reporter may not have a picture editor at all. Desktop digital editing would be done by the journalists/reporters themselves. But however the story is finally constructed, that deadline remains the same.

Viewing the rushes

Ensure that your rushes boxes, sometimes called the 'road tapes', are accurately and precisely labelled. It is easy to misplace them or to mix them up with other tapes in a busy newsroom. View the rushes with an ear and eye to the sound and vision needs of your story. The trick is to let the pictures do most of the talking! A script should explain what we see, guide the viewer, and complement the images.

When you reach the edit suite – and this may be very soon after viewing – explain the basics of the story to the picture editor and how long the final report should be. Never treat a picture editor as someone who just operates the equipment. If you are unsure or new to the job, do tell the picture editor and take advice about what works and what does not. There are some tips to be aware of. It is useful to explain to the editor what you have in mind as an opening shot, and as a closing shot. Pans and zooms which looked so good when you viewed them do not edit well together and often simple static shots are best for news. Often the picture editor may have problems with the sound and this is the most common reason for shots to take longer than expected to edit. Keep a record of time-codes and clock times and the durations of shots or clips from interviewees.

Assuming you have already viewed the rushes, the picture editor will expect your decision about the order and duration of every shot and interviewee clip. Do not simply hand over a piece of paper with time-codes. That should happen only if you really must leave the edit suite because of other duties – probably when a very big story is breaking and it's a case of all hands to the pumps!

Interview extracts (sound-bites)

There can be no firm rule about interview extracts. All news organisations have their own based on programme style. In general the more 'tabloid' or faster-paced, the shorter the interview snippet will be. So the best guidelines probably cannot go beyond three general suggestions:

- Avoid editing sound-bites so tightly that they seem unnatural.
- Make them long enough to register with the audience.
- Use interview extracts to get across interpretation or opinion while you concentrate on the facts.

Building up the story
Take care to ensure the edited story reflects all your fieldwork. View the rushes with the picture editor, checking duration of shots and sequences against the digital time code on the picture.

A poor intro can ruin the best package.

Your Place in the Programme

Some news organisations take remarkably little interest in the later stages of assignments they ask you to cover. No supervision or advice is offered, and you are left to make your own judgement about content and duration. The only support you may get is from colleagues willing to spare a few moments from their own duties to share your problems, in the knowledge that you will reciprocate when the time comes.

Comment, if any, from your superiors is reserved until after what you've done has been aired, and then it tends to be critical rather than complimentary. Unless you make a point of asking directly, the only way you may discover you are doing your job well is because no-one says you are doing it badly.

This is not necessarily a deliberate policy. In fact it is almost a compliment to be trusted to make decisions by yourself. Often the reason is pressure on time and lack of staff. Programme editors simply have too many things to do in the few hours leading to daily transmission, and previewing your three-minute item is one they can do without.

Writing the introduction

Where your news organisation doesn't run to the luxury of separate producers or newswriters, another of your responsibilities as a reporter may be to write an introduction to your own completed package. At the least you may be expected to provide a few ideas in note form.

Either way, the introductory words must be constructed in a way which keeps the audience interested enough to stay tuned in to the report about to follow. Give them as much thought as the rest of your work. Include graphics where they help. Introductions should be complementary and not include facts or phrases immediately repeated in the first paragraph of your report.

One sure way of avoiding this trap is to write a full introduction of, say, three sentences, discard the first two for the presenter to use as the introduction and begin your commentary proper with the third sentence. It works most effectively.

'Musical' news

Finally, an admission of personal prejudice against the use of background music in news items – it is often an easy substitute for natural sound effects, voice-over commentary, or an accompaniment to 'pretty' pictures. All this does is expose the reporter's lack of skill and imagination in finding the right words or natural sound.

Music, unless strictly relevant, should be left where it belongs, in the archives with the cinema newsreels.

Mon Apr 3 16:12

==

John

cam 1 close-up ——————————/A plan to free Britain's motorists

from traffic jams on the roads of

the future has begun to take shape.

The work is being carried out by

the team in charge of a new

computer system which is being

installed in

Map ————————————————/a former stately home in Berkshire

not far from the M-180 link road.

John Johnson has been finding out

the details.

Fitting in to the programme
Introductions should complement the report the viwer is about to see. The 'Computer Traffic' package is preceded by a short script (1) to be read by the presenter, and electronic graphics (2) to add interest. (courtesy Quantel)

Leave time for things to go wrong.

On the Road

In some circumstances you will be surprised to find that it takes longer to plan returning your material to base than it does to gather it in the first place. Even in Europe and the United States, where communications are generally excellent, reporters and their camera crews often face frustration over basic mistakes or accidents which result in delay and missed deadlines.

At your own pace
Wherever possible always allow yourself enough time to do the job as you would wish it to be done. Only you know how long it takes to learn a piece-to-camera or write a commentary. Don't let the approach of hunger, tiredness or fear of offending the camera crew persuade you into a rush job or the acceptance of a performance you suspect is not up to your usual standard. Lunch can wait – the story can't.

The hazards of going live
The revolution which has taken place in television news has put extra pressure on reporters. Live news is something the public is now conditioned to expect – to see events as they happen. When you are asked to 'go live' you will be linked directly to the programme, either in vision and direct to camera, or out of vision as a commentator to the sound and pictures the viewers will witness. This is the thrill and immediacy of television news. There are practical precautions the reporter/commentator can take. You should make sure you know when you expect to perform – and be ready well in advance. Do not go wandering off in search of the latest information and risk not being back in front of camera or behind the microphone in time. There's not much point in having all the latest information if you are not there to deliver it – or, worse, being the subject of an apology: '... Well, we're sorry. We don't seem to be able to get through to our reporter at the moment ...!' When live make sure you have at least three or four vital points to put across, and make sure you have memorised them. Each point will kick-start your brain to help you elaborate. Stick to short sentences. Long monologues make you sound out of breath. Numbers and statistics in a live report can cause problems. These are the most likely things to get wrong in a slip of the tongue – billion, when you meant million, for example. If you really need to quote from notes make sure your notebook is in vision, otherwise you appear to be staring at the ground.

Coping with spectators
Crowds are still attracted by television activity, or by the very events which television seeks to cover live. If they are good-natured but noisy, you can often take control by seeking out the loudest bystanders and give them the responsibility of keeping the rest quiet! Do not give spectators money to shut up. If they are hostile and your instinct tells you that the presence of yourself and the camera could actually encourage violence, then tell base, and then get out.

The hazards of going live
It can be extremely distracting to have spectators watching you report live. At least the crowd on this occasion was not hostile. (courtesy BBC Central Stills)

Few events command genuine interest world-wide.

Covering the World

Some issues and processes assume an international dimension – changes to the global economy, the breakdown of old orders and old certainties, the famine and disease of some countries and the pollution or consumption of others. The war in Bosnia was described by some journalists as the war you could catch a bus ride to. The Gulf War was fought not only in the desert, but in our homes in every news bulletin. The effect of television news is built into the military and diplomatic policy of many governments. Social commentators will provide volumes of research on the news values of the media, but the journalists will maintain that they are primarily interested in those events which will have some direct bearing on the audiences they serve.

Sources

Despite the often-criticised parochialism of television news, coverage of foreign issues does remain an important ingredient. For the big, internationally minded services whose audiences have come to expect same-day coverage of every important happening, it is also usually by far the most expensive part of their news-gathering operations, and every unexpected foreign story of real significance adds another strain to budgets which are frequently already over-stretched.

Television receives foreign news from several main sources:

- Local news services offer coverage of their own domestic events to the international news exchanges, which swap material between member countries over semi-permanent circuits several times a day.
- International wire services or news picture agencies have resident correspondents stationed in or close to most important international centres, and provide a large proportion of the raw material.
- Freelance journalists make their living from serving several outlets, although they may also be paid retainers by their best customers as a means of ensuring that they provide a minimum service.
- Stringers, who owe their first loyalties to the organisations which employ them, are also able to provide material to others on an irregular basis. Both these categories contain people who may not be full-time journalistic practitioners.
- Resident correspondents are based in countries from which the flow of important news is considered regular enough to justify the expense of having staff journalists permanently assigned.
- Foreign bureaux consist of several correspondents and ancillary staff established in particularly important centres where the presence of only a single correspondent would not be sufficient.
- The 'fire brigade' is made up of general reporters who are sent out from home base to cover specific stories, or to back up freelances, stringers or correspondents.
- Other methods of gathering foreign material include the systematic monitoring of foreign broadcasts, often the first accurate source of 'official' news.

100

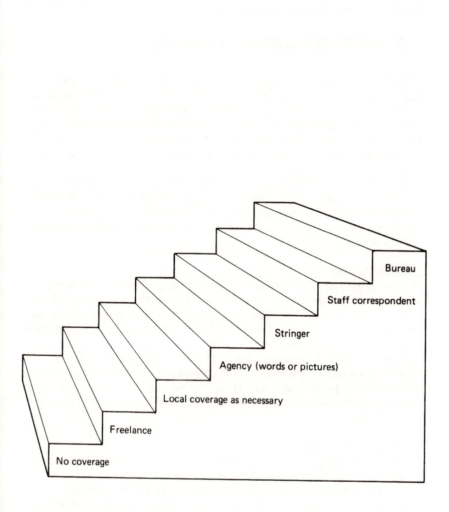

Bureau

Staff correspondent

Stringer

Agency (words or pictures)

Local coverage as necessary

Freelance

No coverage

Steps to world news coverage
News organisations grade their overseas representation according to the importance
they place on an area. But foreign coverage is approximately three times as expensive
as 'home' news, so, at the highest level, sharing bureaux and facilities with
broadcasters from other countries' services can make economic and journalistic sense.

The Foreign Correspondent

Comprehensive news coverage of another country is best achieved by basing a staff journalist – a foreign correspondent – on the spot. The job is usually considered the most glamorous of all reporting assignments. Living in another country as the representative of an overseas news organisation carries with it social as well as professional prestige, and a correspondent who spends some time abroad builds up contacts and sources which ensure that a steady flow of news big and small is sent home.

In countries with dictatorships or totalitarian political regimes, resident correspondents of foreign news organisations are barely tolerated rather than welcomed. Restrictions are placed on their movements and what they can report, and transgressions are met with official warnings, expulsion, imprisonment or worse.

Choosing a base

In days of financial stringency, few television organisations can afford the luxury of having more than a handful of their journalists permanently off base abroad unless they are cost-effective. The areas singled out for this special treatment have to offer a proven or potentially high volume of newsworthy material, and they also have to offer efficient transport and other communications links. London, Washington, Tokyo, Moscow and Paris probably head the list of international capitals in which any news organisation of repute would always wish to be properly represented, but other centres go in and out of fashion according to their political and economic fortunes, and are kept under constant review.

Correspondent costs

The cost of keeping a correspondent anywhere does not end with his or her salary and professional needs. There are personal arrangements to be made for accommodation, transport, perhaps education for the children, and a hundred and one other things which make up a reasonable standard of living. Some correspondents have several countries or whole continents to cover by themselves, and may be expected to leave base temporarily for any part of their 'patch' where a story breaks.

The danger of 'going native'

Even the most respected resident foreign correspondents may have no more than a two- or three-year tenure in the same country, because it is considered that the knowledge and expertise they gain may be out-weighed by the danger of 'going native'. For some, it becomes difficult to remain objective about a social and political scene with which they become too familiar and sympathetic, and it is better for them to move on to another country and start afresh.

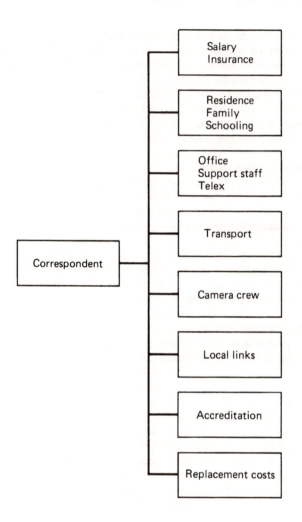

```
                        ┌─────────────────┐
                    ┌───│ Salary          │
                    │   │ Insurance       │
                    │   └─────────────────┘
                    │   ┌─────────────────┐
                    ├───│ Residence       │
                    │   │ Family          │
                    │   │ Schooling       │
                    │   └─────────────────┘
                    │   ┌─────────────────┐
                    ├───│ Office          │
                    │   │ Support staff   │
                    │   │ Telex           │
                    │   └─────────────────┘
┌──────────────┐    │   ┌─────────────────┐
│ Correspondent│────┼───│ Transport       │
└──────────────┘    │   └─────────────────┘
                    │   ┌─────────────────┐
                    ├───│ Camera crew     │
                    │   └─────────────────┘
                    │   ┌─────────────────┐
                    ├───│ Local links     │
                    │   └─────────────────┘
                    │   ┌─────────────────┐
                    ├───│ Accreditation   │
                    │   └─────────────────┘
                    │   ┌─────────────────┐
                    └───│ Replacement costs│
                        └─────────────────┘
```

Foreign correspondent costs
Keeping a staff correspondent on permanent assignment abroad is the most expensive method of covering foreign news. Personal and associated family costs, office accommodation and staffing, and replacement of the correspondent during holiday periods all have to be taken into account.

Enter the Fire Brigade

Inevitably, the number of important foreign stories a good news organisation needs to cover each year includes many in areas not served by a resident correspondent. And while a proportion of these will be reported quite adequately by freelances, stringers or the agencies (see page 100), the rest will probably demand the distinctive approach which can be offered only by a staff journalist. This need is met by despatching one from elsewhere, often home base. So – enter a member of the 'fire brigade', with orders to provide comprehensive coverage, usually within hours of arrival.

Overcoming the first barriers

Working abroad on the shortest assignment can prove a journalistic nightmare for the inexperienced or unwary. Operating in an open society full of helpful people is no more a guarantee of success than operating in one where the democratic process is not developed and foreign reporters are met with suspicion.

Any newcomer to another country is at a disadvantage, and unfamiliar environment, language, customs and living conditions are likely to affect the journalist just as much as anyone else, presenting barriers to be overcome before professional considerations can be brought to bear.

Inoculations and passports

Preparation for foreign assignments should be undertaken with even more care than for domestic ones. Those who expect to be sent abroad at short notice should keep routinely up to date with inoculation against a range of diseases; some countries refuse entry to people without medical certificates proving they are not carriers of infection.

Ensure that passports and visas are valid for long enough to cover outward and return travel. Be alert to the political sensitivites of immigration officials who are on the lookout for the undesirable whose passport bears evidence of visits to countries which their nation boycotts or does not recognise. It pays to be especially cautious in Africa and the Middle East, and experienced, prudent travellers equip themselves with two passports to avoid the embarrassment – or worse – of the mark of a tell-tale rubber stamp.

Journalists with dual nationality can also come into their own at times when it could be a definite drawback to be the holder of a particular passport. In 1982, when the UK and Argentina were briefly in conflict over the sovereignty of the Falkland Islands, a surprising number of journalists who proudly regarded themselves as British suddenly discovered long-lost great-grandmothers in Dublin or Cork and were happily admitted to Buenos Aires bearing Irish passports.

Portable telephone with worldwide capability

Laptop (but a small portable typewriter is still hard to beat in difficult conditions)

Multi-function penknife

Shortwave radio – smallest you can get

Tough shoes – and leather soles are best for comfort in the tropics

Small torch/flashlight

Hat – for Siberian conditions

Sunblock cream

Diahorrea pills

Two passports

Clothes that do not need to be ironed!

A spare for anything personal – glasses, contact lenses, etc.

Trouble-shooting equipment for tough territory
Ideas from some of the most experienced foreign correspondents. You could need all the above while on assignment, depending on climate and circumstances. You might also have to consider the matter of what to use as a bribe at roadblocks or frontier crossings – currency may not be valued. Cheap wristwatches are useful. Alcohol can work wonders in oiling negotiations!

On Foreign Soil

Operating abroad has in many ways become much easier since the introduction of ENG. Previously, a fire brigader covering a story in another country was invariably dependent on the goodwill of the local television station for the processing of film and arrangements for its transmission by landline, microwave or satellite link as an alternative to freighting it home undeveloped and uncut. Delay and frustration were commonplace, especially at times of big stories, when it seemed that half of the world's camera teams were simultaneously demanding facilities from a television station barely equipped to cope with its own programme commitments.

The independent news team
Nowadays the team assigned to a big foreign story will often include a picture editor who travels complete with a mobile editing pack so that the item can be put together on the spot. This is the ideal solution journalistically, but it remains an option open only to those organisations able to afford the cost of flying an entire team and equipment thousands of miles from base.

Setting up
An experienced picture editor can turn virtually any small room into an editing suite within an hour to provide a base for the whole operation. With careful rearrangement of curtains and furniture a hotel room can also double as a simple studio by using the team's camera. All this helps to reduce the pressure on the reporter, who can concentrate on getting the story instead of worrying whether the promised co-operation of another television organisation will be forthcoming and effective.

Unless the team is also carrying its own satellite communications dish or Feedpack – a mobile standards converter through which it is possible to transmit pictures back to base – it will still be necessary to co-operate with the local television station to have the edited material fed home.

Doing your homework
Never take anything for granted when working abroad. The simplest and most obvious matters can bring disaster if overlooked. Make allowance for the difference in time zones between one country and another: remember that a story shot on, say, the PAL 625-line television standard is incompatible with NTSC 525 lines; and that it is no good embarking blindly on a five-minute 'epic' when the assignments desk at home wants and expects a maximum of one and a half.

Camera teams are known to have missed deadlines by confusing local and 'home' times; arrived at a friendly foreign television station with important material on the wrong standard for transmission; and put all their efforts into a lengthy item intended for a programme reduced to a weekend summary.

On foreign soil
Given a little effort, the average hotel room can be turned into a passable imitation of an editing suite (1). Closing the curtains will keep down noise. The picture editor will use headphones instead of loudspeakers and you can record your commentary direct onto the sound track using a 'lip mike' (2). Furniture can be rearranged to create a small 'studio effect' for interviews (3) using the ENG camera.

Communications Satellites

Television reporting may have undergone a revolution since videotape replaced film as the raw material of news gathering: without the communications satellite to speed the material on its way that revolution could not have just been complete.

Journalists have made use of satellite technology since 1962, when Telstar was launched from Florida. The formation of the International Telecommunications Satellite Organisation (Intelsat) followed two years later, providing the impetus for a system which links continents to ensure same-day news coverage from virtually anywhere in the world.

The first satellite in the Intelsat series was known as Early Bird, and 'birding' has become the accepted term for the entire process of transmitting news by satellite. Intelsat, with its headquarters in Washington DC, has a membership in excess of one hundred countries, most of which are represented by their national telecommunications organisations.

How satellites work
Communications satellites are launched into orbit 22,300 miles above earth, at which point they appear to be stationary. In this way global coverage could be achieved, in effect, with one satellite over each of the Atlantic, Pacific and Indian oceans. In fact there are several satellites over each region to cope with the increased traffic – particularly over the busy Atlantic region – and to cover breakdown.

Sound and pictures are sent across continents from one earth station to another via the satellite, which amplifies the signals as well as transmitting them. Television makes only some use of the available communications capacity: the latest generation of Intelsat satellites has a capacity to carry more than 30,000 simultaneous telephone conversations as well as three television channels.

In the late 1980s television moved towards DBS (Direct Broadcasting by Satellite), a method by which signals are directed to individual homes rather than nationally owned ground stations. The satellites have been built for operation by individual governments or commercial consortia.

Satellite news gathering
Such is the need for reliable communications that a number of the richer news organisations have found it worthwhile to invest in their own mobile earth stations. These can be packed into lorries or aircraft to meet the demands of big stories in remote areas, providing instant access to pictures. Self-contained satellite news gathering teams consisting of reporter, camera crew and picture editor, supported by technical staff and facilities, have added an extra flexibility to news gathering. The capital investment is offset partly by bypassing the commercial ground stations in the transmission chain.

108

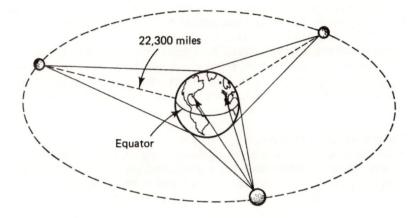

22,300 miles

Equator

The global satellite system
Television signals are beamed 22 300 miles into space to satellites orbiting the earth
There they are received, amplified and transmitted to ground stations on the other side
of the globe. Intelsat, the International Television Satellite Organisation, operates
satellites over the Atlantic, Indian and Pacific Ocean regions, effectively covering
the world.

Assess the risks to 'dissident' interviewees.

Staying Alive

Journalism can be a dangerous business. There are always those who wish to keep their activities hidden and are prepared to go to extraordinary lengths to prevent any attempt at uncovering them. They are not always swayed by arguments about truth, justification, or the national or public interest.

Some regimes get over this problem by simply refusing to open their borders to anyone they consider 'unsympathetic'. Short of illegal entry or posing as a tourist, no reporter can do much about that, and then the consequences of exposure are obvious. Other countries allow in foreign journalists, but impose strict censorship and other conditions which may or may not make it worthwhile being there at all.

It is in these countries, especially, where it is important to be aware that an interviewee encouraged to be outspoken on camera might be 'visited' by the authorities once you are safely back home.

A third category allows journalists in to report what they want – but at their own risk. Parts of Latin America, Africa and the Middle East have proved particularly dangerous in recent years, with wars, civil unrest or general lawlessness making reporting extremely difficult. Death, injury, abduction or imprisonment have befallen hundreds.

The vulnerability of television
Because they do not operate alone, television journalists are conspicuous and therefore especially vulnerable in hostile conditions. The presence of a camera team at a potential trouble-spot is often sufficient to attract unwelcome attention. Depending on the sophistication of those seeking to be disruptive, harassment may range from the minor (a hand over the camera lens or cutting the lead between cameraman and sound operator) to the serious (smashing the equipment) to the very serious (physical attacks on the crew).

Camera teams also find themselves arrested and bundled off for no apparent reason, and although apologies and release may follow fairly swiftly, the damage – removal from the scene – will have been done.

The alternative to arrest is often a demand to hand over such material as has been shot. When faced with this position in democratic countries, the response to police should be to insist that the proper legal process is followed. This is not, however, an approach to be encouraged when the request is made at gunpoint.

Protection for journalists
The International Press Institute has been concerned with the protection of journalists since it was established in 1951, and other professional bodies have also made attempts to present a united front against the harassment and maltreatment of journalists doing their job. Many news organisations issue their own guidelines to staff in dangerous areas.

Red Cross lifeline
Since 1985 the Press Division of the International Committee of the Red Cross in Geneva has operated a 24-hour lifeline for journalists captured, arrested or held in detention while on professional assignment. The line is available for use by the families, editors and professional organisations of journalists in trouble. Address: 17, avenue de la Paix, CH-1202, Geneva, Switzerland. Telephone: (area code 22) 734 6001.

The Journalist's Survival Code

- You are more important than the story. No story is worth your life.
- If you are threatened, get out as fast as you can.
- If authorities can't guarantee your safety, leave the country.
- Never carry a gun or other weapon.
- Never point your finger; it can be mistaken for a gun.
- Know the country, the region and the people involved.
- Know the language at least well enough to identify yourself and to talk to local residents.
- Always carry complete identification papers.
- If you are in an unfamiliar area, travel with other journalists who know it well.
- Know all your journalistic colleagues in dangerous situations. Strangers may not be what they seem.
- Outcries against abuse provide protection. Resist abuse by authorities and always protest (about) such abuse of yourself and other professionals. But don't become abusive yourself.
- Avoid unknown risks. Vague promises of a story often come from persons who can't guarantee your safety.
- Stories in remote locations far from authority and medical assistance present added risk.
- Do not masquerade as other than what you are. It raises suspicions and creates risks for other professionals.
- Under no circumstances accept compensation from or do work for a non-journalistic or government information-gathering intelligence agency.
- A professional must maintain a standard of truth despite risks and dangers. Some stories are worth more risk than others.
- Avoid bias for one side or another. Do not cross the line between journalist and active participant.
- Weigh what you know about the risks against the possible benefits of a story. Often, a story is just as good if covered from a distance.
- Distinguish between risk and present danger. Avoid obvious danger and don't take undue risks. Often discussing this with friends and colleagues can help.
- Avoid reporting from both sides of a conflict if possible. Crossing from one side to the other is always dangerous.

- Always carry a white flag.
- Always use extreme care in selecting competent locals as drivers, guides, etc. Their presence of mind is a protection.
- Mark your car clearly as 'Press' in the local language.
- Use two cars where practical in case one breaks down.
- Never wash your car. Unwanted tampering can be detected easier on a dirty car.
- Talk to local residents as much as possible and listen to their advice.
- Dress appropriately. This will vary. Sometimes you will want to blend into a crowd; at other times you may want obviously not to be one of the group.
- Never wear olive green or anything that makes you look like a soldier.
- Let your desk or editors know where you are at all times, where you are going and when you expect to return.
- Let your colleagues at the hotel know the same thing.
- When confronted by hostile persons, identify yourself in their language and attempt to convey ideas about what you are doing.
- If guerrillas at roadblocks ask you for a 'war tax' give something. It shouldn't be much, but it can avoid unpleasantness.
- Never run checkpoints; never display maps openly.
- Carry a short-wave radio to keep track of developments on the BBC or other reliable stations.
- Think through your mission, how best to get the story. For example, do you risk sniper fire or should you be more circumspect?
- Keep an active mind regarding risks and ask yourself questions.
- All you have in dangerous situations are your wits and knowledge of the area. Your editor and the Geneva Convention normally can't help you.
- Make certain you know the local meaning of symbols like white flags, red flags, whistles, gestures, etc.
- Evaluate your physical characteristics. Don't attempt something you lack stamina to complete.
- Make certain you employer carries insurance that will adequately provide if you are injured or killed.
- Editors should always be aware of the risks reporters or photographers are running. They also bear responsibility and should not push unreasonably.

Reproduced from *Journalists on Dangerous Assignments*, edited by Louis Falls Montgomery, International Press Institute, 1986.

The Anchor

No matter how distinguished or respected reporters may appear to their peers and to the public, there is no doubt that the glamour and fame associated with television journalism attaches more to those who regularly present news or news-related programmes. The curiosity is that the newscaster, newsreader, presenter, anchor – whatever the title – has not always been a journalist. Readers are known to have been hired for their looks or voices and have not necessarily even been invited to make any contribution towards the editorial process, their liberty to change scripts – only after due consultation – being confined to words or phrases they find difficult to say.

The journalist/presenter
The arrival of the journalist as presenter has coincided with new demands created by technological change and the introduction of modern programme formats. Journalistic and presentational skills have become inseparable. Now, when executives look for people able to meet this dual requirement they turn first to their more experienced reporters, some of whom are weary after years of being on the road and are prepared to exchange their globe-trotting for the safety of the studio and elevation to star status. So journalist/presenters are hired not for their looks or voices alone, but also for their experience, and as a consequence are able to command salaries far in excess of the programme editors to whom in theory they may be junior.

Presenter power
Where proper chains of command are not established, collisions of ego are not unknown, usually to the detriment of the programme. Some managements believe that this 'creative tension' makes a positive contribution towards lively journalism. Other organisations do not allow reporters to become presenters for more than short periods, while others try to avoid the problem altogether by making the reporter/presenter the editor, adding executive responsibility for budgets, and the assigning, hiring and firing of staff to the day-to-day editorial decision making. This may be effective policy at one level, but as soon as transmission time approaches and the manager/presenter has to become only the presenter, the difficulties become apparent, leading to the creation of enormous strains on a single person, whatever their talents.

This problem is not likely to surface for the new reporter, but if you have a secret yearning for the presenter's chair, volunteer for a few programmes as a reader at weekends and see if you can establish a reputation as a reliable stand-in. Who knows where that might lead?

In the Studio

The prospect of anchoring a news programme under the bright lights of a television studio in front of millions of critical viewers is enough to make anyone apprehensive.

Although they may never admit it, even the most experienced news presenters suffer an occasional attack of 'butterflies' before a programme. On location there is the possibility of a face-saving second take: in the studio there is no reprieve. The wrong inflection, the slight hesitation or stumble over a word, the sidelong glance or twitch of a facial muscle is a matter for comment and discussion.

Thriving under pressure

Being at the centre of a hectic, live programme may be exactly the right role if you are one of those who thrives on pressure and responsibility.

Accept also that it can be a lonely occupation. You may be expected to operate entirely on your own from a tiny, out-of-town studio equipped with only a remote-controlled camera and lights you switch on yourself to broadcast to the unseen audience.

Glitzy presentation in bigger studios may not offer much more company. You may be asked to read from a computer-driven script-prompting device mounted on robotic cameras, introduce a succession of recorded images played from another part of the building and listen to the disembodied voice of the studio director shouting in your ear. The nearest human contact may be the floor manager standing well out of camera range.

In your own words ...

What you may find most difficult is the idea that what you are reading has been written by someone else. Ten to one you will not be happy with the style or the phrasing. And here it depends how much authority the reader has – either to alter material written by others, or to write it yourself. Even if you wished, it is unlikely that you would be able to write an entire half-hour programme. The concession many programmes make to their journalist/presenters is to allow them to write the headlines, if there are any, or perhaps the opening item.

... and those of others

At the very least the opportunity is likely to occur for you to see every script before it is finalised so that a certain amount of personal authority can be injected. The trick is to encourage others to write in 'your' style right from the beginning or, if that is not possible, to make alterations in a way which retains accuracy and allows the originator of the material to keep some professional pride. Complaints that you have ruined scripts by making alterations without consultation will not enhance your reputation with the rest of the team.

Output

Engineer   Sound   Vision   Studio   Production
            mixer   mixer   director   assistant

In the studio
The television studio can be a lonely place. Instructions to the presenter are fed from a control room probably some distance away. The studio director (1) is in charge of the production team, which may include a production assistant (2), technicians in charge of vision (3) and sound (4), and a senior engineer (5).

115

Sit up straight and don't slouch!

Perfecting Posture

Among the most common faults of those facing the studio television camera is that of poor posture. Somer readers slouch back in their chairs, others – unable to sit squarely – thrust one shoulder forwards in a seemingly aggressive manner which also presents only one eye to the audience. Other readers are so nervous that they sit literally on the seat edge, or slump so round-shouldered that they fill only the bottom of the screen. Still more fidget. All of these habits are distractions. What the viewers want to see is you, the presenter, looking relaxed, confident and assured. Don't let them spend time wondering what is wrong. They will not be able to concentrate on the important matters which you have to tell and show them, and they will become irritated, bored, and switch off.

The wriggle routine
Develop a short routine you go through before you settle down to read a script. First, wriggle yourself comfortably into your chair. If – as in the majority of news-type programmes – there is a desk between yourself and the camera, make sure the chair is at a height which suits your physique and not that of the giant who used it last. If it cannot be adjusted, ask for another.

Check that you are exactly far enough away to put down and pick up your papers naturally, without stretching. Don't worry about the cameras. It is the responsibility of the production staff to move them if necessary. Above all, do not allow yourself to be rushed.

If you still have a tendency to slump, try sitting on your coat tail to keep your back straight. If you are not in the habit of wearing a coat, write in large letters at the top of your script 'sit up straight'.

Using a clipboard
The more informal the programme, the more difficulties there often are for the presenter, who is likely to have to cope with a wad of script pages in one hand and a favourite pen or pencil in the other. If there are no desks or tables within easy reach, cross your legs and rest the papers on your knee. If there are many pages do not risk getting them out of order or spilling them on the floor – you don't want to be scrambling among the camera cables just before an important interview.

The best tip is to keep your sheets on a clipboard, turning them over with the hand which holds the pen. Sheets can be discarded out of shot during the programme.

Formality and informality
Posture is important: try sitting on your coat tails to keep your back straight (1). If there's no desk you'll have to balance your script on your knee, but it can be difficult to sit elegantly (2). Informal sets have easy chairs and tables (3).

A useful tool.

The Script Prompter and How to Use It

One of the great innovations to help performers improve their presentation technique is the prompting device which gives the impression that the words are being spoken from memory. Audiences are less likely to be fooled or surprised by this than they used to be, and prompter techniques have found their way into speech delivery. If you watch the wider shots at a political or public conference you might see two transparent plates on top of thin posts on either side of the speaker. It is these which project the words – seen by the orator, but invisible to the audience. They add a professional touch as well as giving confidence and credibility to all forms of speech-making.

Beyond the idiot board
Script prompting hardware has improved considerably since the early days of 'idiot boards' – handwritten cards or sheets held below or just to one side of the camera. This technique was followed by long narrow sheets of paper onto which the script was typed and then projected by mirrors onto the front of each camera lens without obscuring the shot. All prompter systems are now electronic and can appear in front of the newsreader at the touch of a button.

Avoid the shifty look
The most important thing for the presenter to be aware of is that the narrowness of the script on the prompter means that only three or four lines can be seen at a time, and each line may contain only four or five words. Make a point of trying to read the words from the centre of the screen rather than from side to side. Do feel free to move your head and body weight slightly from time to time. It looks more natural. It is also natural to look down occasionally to consult your hard copy, the paper script on your desk. The viewer needs to be reassured that some facts – figures or direct quotations in particular – are not somehow being conjured up from memory. The trick is to look down as if refreshing the memory, then look up again and continue presenting from the prompter. Always ensure that the page in hard copy form in front of you is the same page on the prompter.

If you have never presented using a prompter, make sure you get some practice before you go on air. Even a few minutes is useful. Best of all, borrow a director and studio for an hour or two, try it several times, and also practise a disaster – that moment when the prompter breaks down and you have to get your head down to the hard copy.

118

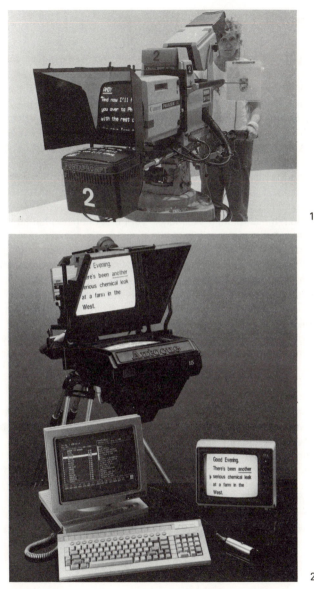

The electronic prompter
(1) Reader's eye view (courtesy EDS Portaprompt). (2) Prompting systems linked with newsroom computers allow script changes and updates to be made without writers leaving their desks for the studio. (courtesy Autocue)

Talkback

Another part of the art of presenting in the studio comes with listening to what is going on in the control room. 'Talkback' gives you direct contact with the director or editor, so instructions before or during any programme item can be given easily. Using the desk telephone always looks so theatrical.

Almost every regular studio performer of any status is now equipped with a tiny, snug-fitting personal earpiece, rather like a hearing-aid. The other end is fitted to a long cable which eventually plugs into an electrical socket at the back of the desk.

You may find it impossible to use this device at first: it's rather like the childish game of trying to pat your head and rub your stomach at the same time. It takes practice to concentrate on speaking clearly while people in another room are chattering excitedly in your ear, often about matters which do not strictly concern you.

On the other hand it is a splendidly useful means of communication. For example, many readers like to be counted in and out of video inserts, relying on the warning voice of the production assistant in their ear, and there is more than one star television performer who has cause to be thankful for this mechanism which allows an astute producer in the control room to regularly whisper the line of questioning to be followed during live interviews.

Although the word 'talkback' implies a two-way process, the only way you are able to talk back to the control room is by using the desk microphone. If you do, make sure it's not 'live', during transmission.

The floor manager

If you prefer, the distractions of talkback can be avoided by switching it off during transmission and putting your faith in the floor manager, who is linked by headset and microphone to the control room.

The floor manager stands out of camera range but near enough to be able to relay the studio director's instructions by hand signals. In many cases these may consist of nothing more complicated than a series of rehearsed finger movements to denote the time remaining on a video insert. In other cases the floor manager has an essential role in the progress of live interviews or other items which need to be kept strictly to their planned duration, and so circular 'wind-up' and 'cut-throat' actions are used as time runs out.

The floor manager
The floor manager acts as the link between the control room and the presenter in th
studio. (courtesy BBC Central Stills)

Too cosy a partnership will seem phoney.

Presenters in Partnership

The preference for news-related programmes to be fronted by one, two or more presenters is influenced as much by fashion as by journalistic needs. Changes are quite often made as part of the acceptable, periodic revision of format or style made by all long-running factual programmes, and a decision to switch from, say, solo to dual presentation – or vice versa – is treated as one element of a revamp or re-launch likely to include the introduction of new sets, titles, music and graphics.

Sometimes it goes beyond the cosmetic: a multi-presentation format may be driven by the need to base anchors in different centres, to inject pace and variety, or to relieve the pressures on a single journalist fronting longer, technically complicated programmes.

Attracting the audience
Male–female partnerships are particularly popular with audiences, and other combinations intended to broaden the viewing base include teams which have an age or racial mix.

Dividing the work
Where presenters are in tandem the aim is usually to split the work more or less equally (some insist on a minimum share of on-air time being written into their contracts). As a standby or novice presenter it is unlikely that you would be in a position to make similar demands, but from the outset it is worth clarifying the extent of your contribution: whether you are expected to conduct interviews during the programme, or read alternate segments, scripts or voice-overs. This is a wise precaution, as it is not unknown for 'junior' presenters to find themselves disadvantaged by their established star partners, who feel threatened and attempt to influence programme managements to divide the reading spoils in a way which gives them the hard news and serious political interviews and leaves you with all the soft items.

Formality and informality
Journalists never cease to argue about the degree of informality which ought to exist between presenter partnerships on air. Of course it depends on so many things, one being the time a programme is being transmitted. Breakfast news-show styles tend to be the most relaxed, with formality seeming to increase progressively through the day.

My own view is that presenters should convey a friendly yet crisp and efficient impression to the audience without descending to the jocularity and byplay which rarely comes across as anything but contrived.

If you are encouraged to be informal, be aware that on occasions it can seem callous and badly out of place. The end of a programme made up of a catalogue of death and disaster is no time for merry quips between presenters.

In tandem
Team presentation calls for the audience to believe that two people are sharing the same studio, even though they may be seen together only briefly at the opening and closing of a programme. For this it is essential to maintain an interest when it is not your turn. As your partner finishes an item the camera should find you looking in his or her direction. The hint of a head turn towards the audience will add to the impression that the two of you are working together.

Play fair by your interviewee.

Studio Interviewing (1)

The arrival of the journalist/presenter or anchor has meant a broadening of the role beyond the straightforward reading to camera. Live studio interviews within news programmes are no longer the novelties they once were, and anyone aspiring to a permanent studio-based role needs to develop the technique.

The difference between interviewing on location and in a studio is more than a matter of the difference between a live broadcast and an edited recording. Transferred to the confines of a studio, almost any interview appears to take on a more confrontational nature, created in part by the technical paraphernalia of cameras and lights, which add an air of unreality to the proceedings.

The interview's test
Your skill in interviewing live is tested to the full by the need to:
● Make the interview flow.
● Extract the best from the subject as a duty to the audience.
● Avoid making grammatical or editorial errors which cannot be corrected.
● Cover all the relevant ground before the interview runs its allotted duration.
This task is rarely made easier by the inteview subject. Canny, ring-wise politicians have the ability to make mincemeat of interviewers if they have a mind to do so.

Part of your difficulty with these interviews is a natural tendency to play fair by your visitors and not to appear aggressive, so those who have developed the infuriating but devastating technique of ignoring your questions and answering their own can be very hard to put in their place.

An added drawback is that the public usually relishes the sight of an inter-viewer on the retreat. Equally, many big-name interviewers become as famous as those who regularly make the headlines, and the gladiatorial nature of an interview between people who socialise off-screen can sometimes be no more than play-acting. That much is often made clear by their behaviour towards each other before or after the event.

Interview one plus one
Most live interviews in the studio are between two people. The set should be designed so they face more or less opposite. If they sit side-by-side they will be looking towards each other in profile and the audience will seem to be excluded. Camera positioning should be such that the subject talks to both the interviewer and the audience. This is best achieved with a three-camera set-up: one trained on the interviewer, one on the interviewee, and one on a two-shot of both.

Interview one plus one
A three-camera set-up. Camera 1 is trained on the interviewee, Camera 2 on you and Camera 3 covers both participants in a two-shot.

125

Be involved: don't let yourself become a spectator.

Studio Interviewing (2)

Interview one plus two
Conducting an interview with two people is obviously twice as tricky as with one, chiefly because of the need to play fair by each participant. For even if the two interviewees are theoretically on 'the same side', it is important that both should have their say, as much for the sake of good television as for balance.

It is not always enough to ask each the same question in turn: this can be far too slow and predictable. The interviewer's skill comes in being able to pick up one answer and use it to move the subject smoothly forward, so by the end of the allotted time a satisfactory amount of ground has been covered and a range of interviews heard.

Firmness counts
Where the participants have strongly opposing views it is important not to let the interview become a succession of claims and counter-claims. Resist the temptation to deliberately light the fuse and retire to enjoy the fireworks. Although a good row between interviewees can produce spectacular viewing, it is just as likely to degenerate into childishness which quickly becomes very boring. Far better not to let things get out of control from the beginning. Firmness is essential, otherwise you may find yourself a virtual spectator as the 'ball' is batted across from one side to the other. Assert your authority as politely as possible, making sure you do not appear to be in favour of one or other of the arguments.

Setting up the studio for the one plus two may be less problematical than may seem obvious. If three cameras are available, one can cover both speakers in single shots if they sit opposite you side-by-side. But it is important to have separate microphones for each person.

Interview one plus more than two
It is arguable whether multi-participant interviews are of much editorial value within a news-type programme of limited duration. There never seems to be enough time available to give everyone a decent hearing. From a production point of view, too, such interviews can be difficult unless a proper set has been built to accommodate large numbers.

On the rare occasions when you are faced with interviews of this type, take time out from your research to help advise on seating arrangements. Without preparation, the production team will be unable to direct the cameras and microphones at the right people when they speak.

One plus two
An unusual combination: one interviewer and two interviewees. Sky News, recruited politicians with opposing views – Norman Tebbit (Conservative) and Austin Mitchell (Labour) – to quiz guests for a regular programme. (courtesy Sky News)

Live interview dos

- DO know your subject. There's no better way of keeping your interviewee's respect and interest.

- DO prepare your questions in advance.

- DO listen to the answers and be ready with supplementaries.

- DO wait for a breath pause or natural break in speech flow if you have to interrupt.

- DO keep the inteviewee to the subject under discussion.

- DO be persistent if you can't get answers to legitimate questions. But judge when enough is enough.

- DO not be tempted to defer to an interviewee who is famous or powerful.

- DO nurture the nervous. If an interviewee has a tendency to avoid eye-contact ask a direct question to attract greater attention.

- DO give time for thought: silence can be telling.

- DO keep control of your facial expressions. Raising your eyebrows or nodding your head could be interpreted as comment.

- DO remember that it's your job to ask questions, not to take part in a debate.

- DO avoid putting words into people's mouths: 'What I think you are trying to say, Mr Bloggs, is ...'

- DO remember who you are interviewing. 'Drying' is quite natural under pressure. Write the subject's name and title on your script.

- DO listen to control-room talkback.

- DO try to pace yourself so the interview comes to a smooth conclusion.

- DO keep to the time you have been allotted. Finishing earlier or later than planned will disturb programme balance.

- DO remember you have the privilege of being able to ask the questions the average person would like to put, given the opportunity. You are representing the audience, no-one else.

Live interview don'ts

- DON'T assume the audience shares any specialist knowledge you may have.

- DON'T stick rigidly to prepared questions and ignore the answers.

- DON'T make statements. The interviewee may not know when to answer.

- DON'T make statements of your own in the form of questions. You aren't taking part in a debate.

- DON'T as a rule refer to interviewees by their first names: it can sound patronising.

- DON'T talk at the same time as your subject.

- DON'T bicker or lose your temper under provocation.

- DON'T be intimidated by an overbearing interviewee.

- DON'T bully or hector an interviewee who is unimportant or inarticulate.

- DON'T go easy on someone just because you sympathise.

- DON'T jump in with another question if an interviewee hesitates: allow a few seconds for recovery.

- DON'T let your own opinions come through. No-one is interested.

- DON'T respond to answers with 'I see', 'yes' or semi-audible grunts. It could be habit-forming.

- DON'T ask leading questions: '… and then I believe you saw the fire-engine coming round the corner at sixty miles an hour …'

- DON'T enter into little intimacies or conspiracies with the interviewee to the exclusion of the viewer. 'You and I both remember what happened after that wonderful meal in Paris … but we'd better not talk about that, ha, ha.'

- DON'T ignore the floor-manager's signals. They are there to help you.

- DON'T cut your interviewee off with a brusque 'Sorry, we are out of time.'

- DON'T FORGET that you have the privilege of being able to ask the questions the average person would like to put, given the opportunity. You are representing the audience, no-one else.

Tricky Customers and 'Spin Doctors'

Although the advantages might appear to be on the side of the professional interviewer operating on familiar ground there is a common belief among journalists that the initiative is passing to experienced interviewees. Many of them know how to exploit the medium. Many of them are trained by experienced broadcasters and there is no reason why they should not be entitled to know more about the way television and interviews operate. They are coached and drilled to deal with certain questions. Advice is offered on dress, posture and delivery. An aide to a politician once asked a well-known interviewer how his boss could do better in his television interviews. 'Tell him to just be himself. Be natural,' was the advice. 'That's what I'm afraid of,' was the reply. Successful politicians rarely complain about the media – they use it. There is the balance: the interviewee may bring pressure on the interviewer or editor to ensure he or she is seen in the best light, or it could all be interpreted as unjust and blatant news management.

The tactics, and 'spin doctors'
Some pressures are simple and unsubtle. This usually consists of conditions laid down before an interviewee will agree to appear at all. To impose extra pressure the conditions may be imposed just minutes before the interview is to take place. This leaves the journalist with a simple option – agree, or face a last-minute walkout! Only the circumstances can answer that one – is the interview worth it?

The people who form the buffer, or link, between politicians and the media have become more subtle: background briefings to favoured reporters, double-edged comments provided strictly off-the-record, leaking policy just to test public opinion, and then denying it all if the public does not like it. These are only a few of the techniques being used in the looking-glass world of political policy, business and the media. The good news is that everyone involved usually knows the rules. The reporter should know what is really going on, and needs to distinguish between rumour, comment, gossip, and the real facts. Another technique is to actually keep off the screen anyone regarded as a poor performer or poor representative of the company/political party/pressure group, either because he or she is untelegenic, a poor speaker, or both, or just boring. A sad paradox is that some of the best minds on any subject may frequently be 'unavailable' when you contact a press office.

Before the interview

These are among the conditions interviewees are known to have laid down before agreeing to be interviewed:

SOLO INTERVIEWS
Non-appearance unless:
- 'live' transmission
- guaranteed position in programme
- duration agreed
- questions submitted in advance
- approval of interviewer
- preview of any other contributions
- no editing of recording
- preview and approval of recording before transmission

MULTIPLE INTERVIEWS
Non-appearance unless:
- veto over other participants
- guarantee of minimum time
- guarantee of the 'last word'
- veto over seating arrangements

Other ploys:
- threats to leave before inteview
- intimidation of the interview

During the interview
- evasion of questions
- insistence on making statements
- interruptions
- calling by Christian name
- simulated anger
- walk-out

After the interview
- complaint about treatment
- insistence on apology
- insistence on vetting recording
- threat of legal action

Difficult interviewees
It is quite legitimate for interviewees to lay down conditions before they agree to appear, although be on your guard against anything which smacks of news manipulation. In the end it depends on how badly you want the inteview. But once you have agreed to any conditions, stick to them.

Interviewee on the Attack

It would be wrong to assume that all interviews for television are arranged with mutual respect and a proper regard for the needs of both sides, bearing in mind that in the end they are providing a service for the viewer. Alas, it is not like that at times. Interminable wrangling over seemingly trivial detail goes on behind the scenes before the participants ever reach the studio, although it has to be emphasised that what we are considering here are mainly news-related or potentially contentious items and not talk shows or other forms of entertainment interview.

Softening up the interviewer

Sometimes a strong performance on television does wonders for a politician's waning popularity – as much with their peers as with the voter – and it is understandable that they should try to seize any psychological advantage which offers itself. Don't be caught off-guard by pre-interview tactics. These might include half-joking, half-serious criticism of your past work, complaints about real or imagined transgressions on the part of colleagues or your parent news organisation.

Ignoring the question

At some time or other during an interview of significance, the experienced interviewee is likely to introduce the favourite yet effective ploy of ignoring your question and answering one of their own. Fortunately, most signal what's coming well in advance with a reply which says, in essence: 'I really think you're missing the point. What's far more important ...'

Other interviewees do not bother with such subtleties. Instead they deliberately go off at a tangent or create an impenetrable verbal smoke-screen through which it is practically impossible to judge whether the question has been answered at all. If you are not careful the interview can be beyond control in no time.

Be patient. Repeat the question and, if necessary, say why you are doing so. As long as you are courteous and don't appear to be over-zealous, the audience will be on your side.

Other ploys

Another favourite ploy is to patronise the interviewer by using his or her first name. It is extremely difficult to ask hard questions of someone who seems anxious to be friendly and co-operative. Counter this by using the appropriate honorific.

Post-interview troubles

Even if an interview has apparently gone well, it is no guarantee against unwelcome complaint from those who have had second thoughts about what they should or should not have said. Protests that a recorded interview has been distorted through editing should be taken seriously.

Tricky customers
An imaginary television interview in Three Acts.

BACKGROUND: the government's treatment of the economy has hit a rough patch and there are calls for the resignation of those responsible for policy. One senior politician whose position is known to be vulnerable has agreed to a live interview on a daily current affairs programme.

ACT ONE: BEFORE TRANSMISSION
(Scene, an anteroom. Politician is being attended to by a make-up artist while discussing the subject with interviewer, an experienced television reporter. They know each other well.)

POL. Now Bill, you know I'm always happy to co-operate, but you're not going to ask any trick questions, are you?

INT. Well John, obviously I am going to have to ask you generally about the state of the economy and then, more specifically, whether you think there will have to be a change of direction. You know your position is a bit vulnerable.

POL. You're telling me! But don't overstate it. No-one's going to thank you for trying to undermine confidence in what we are doing. Just the same, I don't see why I should sacrifice my political career for the sake of some incompetent computer programmer.

INT. Come on, you know they'll look after you. Anyway, I'm going to have to ask the question.

POL. (gloomily). I daresay. But I don't promise to answer.

ACT TWO: IN THE STUDIO
(The interview is under way.)

INT. Mr Jones, the government's own figures show that things aren't going as well as it had forecast. What do you think has gone wrong?

POL. Well, Bill, you and I know the question which should really be addressed is why the previous administration allowed the situation to get so far out of hand it has taken this long to get matters under control.

INT. Isn't it that the situation was being remedied but that you have simply been blown off course?

POL. If you knew anything about economics you'd know that even the most effective policies and the strongest economies are affected by industrial demand and trading patterns in the rest of the world. Surely you'll accept we've made tremendous advances in the past few years.

INT. Mr Jones, what's your reply to those critics inside the government who don't accept that advances have been made and say it is time to introduce new ideas and new people to implement them?

POL. I told you before we began this interview, Bill, that I was not going to answer that question should you put it to me. But I see that as usual the media is not interested in issues, only the unfounded gossip and rumour to do with personalities.

INT. Mr Jones, I'll put it this way. Do you think it is right for the country's economic policy to be in the hands of those in whom some members of the government appear to have lost confidence?

POL. Bill, we are both old hands at this game. It is quite irresponsible of you to go on attempting to ask a question to which I have already given an answer.

INT. But you have refused to answer it, haven't you?

POL. I have answered your question by saying that I am not going to comment on rumour and speculation about my position. So I suggest you change the subject …

ACT THREE: AFTER THE INTERVIEW
(Scene, the hospitality room.)

POL. (cheerily). Well, I think that went rather well Bill, don't you? Thanks. Now, what about that drink …

Audience Participation

Most traditional news-type programmes are serious affairs conducted within the confines of some kind of studio. The public 'out there' is kept on the other side of the television set.

But some of the most charismatic and experienced presenter/reporters who have demonstrated an ability to meet more taxing challanges are invited to host shows in which the participation of an audience is an essential ingredient.

'Panel' programmes which lend themselves to this form of treatment are held in studios or sizeable halls. They are usually fairly relaxed and informal, although the topics they cover – social and environmental issues, health, politics, for example – are serious enough. Each tries to offer something unique in the way of presentation, but the format is now pretty well established and only cosmetic differences are readily apparent.

Programme format

A typical format for one of these programmes consists of two or more groups chosen by the producer or editor for their opposing views, and an audience made up of supporters and neutrals. Questions may be prearranged or come spontaneously from the studio/hall audience or viewers. You may be seated on a platform at one end, facing the audience, or the 'stage' may be located in the middle as if in a theatre in the round.

As the host, it is up to you to allow the main players to espouse their cause (within reason), score points off each other, answer the audience's questions positively, and entertain at the same time. You also have to intervene on occasions to 'referee', seek clarification, chide the question side-steppers, take a firm grip on speakers who attempt to hog the proceedings, and – unless it is 'timeless' – be conscious of the clock.

Be prepared

These programmes are transmitted live, some recorded 'as live' without editing. Others are recorded an hour or so before transmission to allow trimming to time. They are intended to be as much entertainment as good journalism, so approach them in that spirit.

If the programme is meant to reflect current topics, be up to date on what is important. Most journalists invariably are, though even the best can be caught out at times. At the minimum, preparation should consist of a few newspaper clippings put aside for possible use in an emergency. Research the main characters before the programme. If it is one of a series, you may expect to meet the main participants over a meal at which the broad outline of subjects can be discussed. It provides an opportunity for the less experienced to relax without spoiling spontaneity.

Audience participation
Audiences have an integral part in some programmes. The test for the host is to
keep the questions and answers flowing and not to let any one person dominate
the proceedings. 'Kilroy', this programme, is hosted by a former politician,
Robert Kilroy-Silk. (courtesy BBC Central Stills)

Take interest in what the caller has to say.

Phone-ins

Phone-ins tend to be thought of as a recent popular phenomenon. Although it is a technique more appropriate to radio, where hours of cheap programming can be obtained by asking listeners to ring in (often at their own expense) on all manner of subjects, phone-ins have a long history of exposure on television as well. (BBC Archives record a television phone-in for a Party Political Broadcast in July, 1954).

Series of phone-in programmes have been established, many a skilful mix of part studio-based, part telephone questioning. Politics, social and consumer affairs, and listeners' letters are just a few of the topics which lend themselves readily to the treatment, and once you have been enrolled as a host, voluntarily or otherwise, you are likely to find yourself in charge of lengthy live programmes, frequently in the small hours.

Achieving balance
The simplest phone-ins are those which find you alone, fielding calls from the public on some stated topic. In others you will have to cope with a guest or two, a studio audience, and a succession of incoming calls. The skill here is to juggle all elements, keeping the programme flowing in the gaps between calls.

Probably you will have help behind the scenes. Potential contributors speak first to a researcher/producer about the point they wish to raise. In this way repetition is avoided, a balance can be kept between arguments, and new or associated topics introduced. This is also an early warning against callers likely to let loose a stream of abuse or obscenities on the air. Some programmes have a built-in recording device which delays the question long enough for someone to intercept. Bona fide callers are asked to wait or are telephoned back when their turn comes.

Concentrate on the caller
Your role is to act as go-between, interposing when necessary to ensure the caller receives a proper answer. Some contributors become tongue-tied the moment they are invited to put their question, and you should come to the rescue, interpreting or clarifying as the need arises. The caller must not be allowed to seem foolish or be left uncertain about when to speak. Contributors' names are probably fed to you through the earpiece, or on a television monitor out of sight of the viewing audience, but make a habit of writing down who each caller is, where he or she comes from, and the gist of the question. It might save embarrassment. Allow supplementaries and try not to cut people off abruptly. Thanking a caller politely for their contribution is a neat way of telling them their time has run out.

When Things Go Wrong

Don't the viewers love it. There's nothing more likely to grab the attention of the audience than a foul-up on air, and it's always funny in a newsroom as well – so long as it happens to someone else. The natural disasters of television news include computer systems breaking down, and then the editor or presenter wants to know if anyone in the room can use a manual typewriter. Satellite links that worked perfectly in the technical line-up develop mysterious faults while on air. A report might have sound but no pictures, or pictures but no sound, or the right pictures and the wrong sound, or vice versa. Then, of course, there is the electronic prompting device for the news presenter … which is why they have hard copies of the script in front of them.

The human element presents the public with slipping contact lens, wagging fingers at the bottom of the screen, coughs and sneezes, and presenters being caught eating a chocolate bar. A production error on-air can mean that a shot intended of one presenter on Camera One can be replaced by the shot of the other presenter on Camera Two (close-up of other presenter picking his lunch out of his teeth). Even before we are on-air there is plenty to go wrong: scripts written too late to make their deadline, reports which are too long, or too short, and disrupt the planned duration of a programme, videotape delivered by couriers to the wrong address, and taxi drivers taking interviewees to the wrong television company. A camera crew in Paris looking for the offices of the police agency, Interpol, was sent to the premises of the Interpol dry cleaners!

Beware intruders
In this age of direct action and protest about minority rights, some intruders can evade security and chain themselves to a camera at the start of a live broadcast. When this happened during a live news bulletin the main presenter calmly continued as if nothing had happened, while the other presenter muffled the sound of the demonstrator with the seat of his trousers. Not all visitors are human. An American news anchor shared the studio with a wasp. Millions of viewers watched him being stung on the cheek.

Keep calm
The only thing to do when catastrophe strikes is to keep calm. Apologies sometimes seem in order, although one school of thought says it is pointless to draw attention to some minor technical fault that the non-expert viewer would probably not notice. At the other extreme it is foolish to ignore a succession of obvious calamities by pretending they have not happened. Usually the studio control room will come to the rescue with instructions through your earpiece or, in some cases, the emergency telephone on the desk. Quite often the common sense approach is to go on to the next item as soon as possible while the technicalities are sorted out behind the scenes.

But the worst thing presenters can do is to give the impression that it is somehow nothing to do with them and what has gone wrong with the programme is the result of inefficiency elsewhere. That is unforgivable.

137

Last Words on Interviewing

And finally ... remember interviewees are your guests. The way they are treated will determine their attitude towards you and your organisation, and whether – if they are worth cultivating – they are likely to accept a future invitation to appear. It's of benefit to you that they turn up at the right place at the right time. Do not invite interviewees to appear unless you genuinely intend to use them. It is discourteous in the extreme.

Inevitably, there will be occasions when editorial considerations mean 'dropping' at the last moment a guest who has taken considerable trouble to join you. Apologise profusely.

To pay or not to pay?
Guests who take part in news programmes do not usually expect to be paid, although you cannot assume everyone is able to give up their time for nothing. If an interviewee would otherwise be out of pocket it is not unreasonable to offer a small 'disturbance fee' by way of compensation, travelling expenses, or company transport.

Looking after your guest
Do not ignore interviewees when they arrive. If you cannot meet the guest yourself, make it a rule to have someone available to guide them to the studio or waiting room. Let them know what is happening and when they are expected to appear. Offer hospitality: it need be no more than a cup of coffee.

On the air
Be polite, certainly, but do not overdo the verbal greetings. They are inclined to slow down the proceedings. Some nervous interviewees cannot stop talking: when you want to interrupt, make sure they see you lean forward. Others look away when answering. Proper chair positioning will help: otherwise ask a direct question which will make them look at you. Ensure fidgety interviewees are not given swivel chairs. They will probably swivel out of shot.

Illustrating the interview
If you intend to illustrate the interview with graphics, video, or items brought in by the guest (this often happens with magazine programmes) be sure there is time to prepare: the studio will need to set up separate camera shots or lighting changes. If there is any chance illustrations may not appear at the right time or seem out of place – forget them.

How you say goodbye ...
... is as important as how you say hello. You don't have to say 'thank you' on screen, but make sure you do privately afterwards. Then, if it is possible, offer hospitality and return transport.

138

Looking after your guests
Studio interviewees may be difficult to stop talking. If you don't want to interrupt them in full flight, leaning forward (1) should indicate your intention. If it falls within your responsibility to position studio guests, make sure fidgets are not seated in swivel chairs. They might swivel out of shot (2).

Documentaries

Television documentaries present journalists with opportunities to explore subjects in greater depth and length than is normal with news or news-related programmes. More than that, some are 'signed', allowing the reporter to set aside the impartiality demanded of everyday programming in favour of a rarely expressed personal view.

Shape and content

The documentary has no set agenda, so shape, content and duration are open to individual interpretation. Its scope is considerable, and that is why so many imaginative reporters, tramlined by the constraints of straight news journalism, gleefully seize any chance to involve themselves in documentary-making. Others are uncomfortable with the freedom on offer and are irritated by the comparative slowness of the production process, allied to the lack of editorial responsibility they may be given.

This is because the driving force is usually the producer, who is likely to spend several weeks researching a subject before a decision is taken whether to go ahead with it. The reporter may be brought in only at the tail-end to conduct prearranged interviews and to voice scripts written by other people, but how much involvement there is depends on the nature of the programme and its resources. Makers of series – even the most prestigious ones – are not necessarily assigned their own reporter, relying instead on presenters contracted programme by programme.

Documentary production

Documentary-making is usually altogether a more formal activity than 'news', a fact reflected in the size of the production team. Staffing levels are laid down according to national or local management and union agreements, so a typical documentary team working on location might consist of six people, excluding the reporter, whose titles and responsibilities will vary according to custom and practice.

The leader is probably the producer/director, who is in overall charge, combining the financial, editorial and creative responsibilities separated in feature film work. The production assistant may double as researcher as well as undertaking all detailed pre-production organisation, including making arrangements for the team's travel. On location she – as it usually is – keeps track of continuity, script and content. The camera operator works with the producer/director on the composition and framing of each shot, the business of handling the camera itself and loading the film being the responsibility of the assistant camera operator. In the same way, the sound recordist may have an assistant or second sound recordist to look after the equipment and 'slate' every shot with the clapperboard. Where necessary, the team is completed by an electrician, whose range and power of lights comfortably exceeds those used in news, and who may be joined by an assistant for particularly big or uncomplicated productions.

Six stages in documentary-making

Stage 1
RESEARCH
& PLANNING

Stage 2
BRIEF OUTLINE
TREATMENT

Stage 3
SHOOTING SCRIPT

Stage 4
FILMING

Stage 5
EDITING

Stage 6
COMMENTARY
WRITING

Documentary structure
Documentary-making calls for a disciplined approach: in some cases the shape, content and script are decided in detail in advance. The aim is to sustain interest throughout a film lasting anything from about fifteen minutes to an hour or more, and with careful planning it is possible to create peaks of interest at set intervals.

Despite the digital revolution, some filmcraft still exists.

Using Film

Digital video cameras have brought mobility and flexibility in the highly competitive world of television news, but there still remains pockets of film craft where speed is not a priority. Documentary makers will always experiment with digital cameras and digital sound acquisition, but many maintain a tradition of shooting longer form documentary on 35 mm film, which is preferred for its picture quality and the precision of manual editing. Some picture editors say that the physical handling of the film enhances their creative instincts in a way electronic or digital editing does not. Television news reporters are only likely to see real film if it comes from an archive, and to use that in part of a report it would have to be transferred into a modern format for editing.

Film technique
Before the lightweight video revolution of the late 1970s, the manufacturers of newsfilm had introduced a 16 mm cine equivalent of the amateur photographer's 35 mm colour transparency, an original positive for projection but without the need to print. Documentary makers, however, have tended to stick to the more conventional negative–positive process in which the first viewing is made from a print of the rushes – unedited raw material – and the original is stored under laboratory conditions to keep it free from dust, scratches or accidental mishandling during editing. Only after the rushes have been assembled, first into a rough cut and then into a final fine cut, is the original negative produced and edited exactly to match.

Sound
The most commonly used sound system in documentary filming is known as double system (otherwise separate magnetic) or synchronous sound (sync sound). Here the camera operator takes the pictures while the recordist captures the sound on a high-quality recorder using quarter-inch magnetic tape. Camera and recorder work separately but are linked electronically to maintain synchronism. In operation the start of each shot is indicated by use of a clapperboard, although sometimes it is more convenient to make the mark with an inverted 'end board'. Once filming is complete, the film is developed separately and the quarter-inch tape re-recorded onto a ferrous oxide surface.

Using video with film
Although they might have a preference for film, producers and directors often make practical use of electronic technology. Rushes are easily transferred to home video format for examination and review at leisure. In this way preliminary decisions about the shape and content can be made without wasting valuable operational resources. 'Off-line' editing, an intermediate assembly of the video sound and pictures, may also take place at this point, providing the picture editor with an accurate guide from which the original negative can be cut.

Camera loaded
with 16 mm mute film

Clapperboard
to check sync.

Tape recorder
1/4 tape

Film to processing
tape to re-recording
on to 16 mm track

Film

Sound track

Editing

Film sound
Many documentary makers use film in preference to videotape. The double system
(also known as sync sound or sepmag) uses a separate tape machine to record the
sound synchronously with the film.

1   2   3

Film editing equipment
(1) Editing machine, (2) film bin on which the selected shots are pinned in sequence,
and (3) the tape joiner. Cut film is butted together with transparent sticky tape.

143

The Reporter as Commentator

With the right voice, a gift for economy and carefully chosen words, and the charming turn of phrase which makes journalism a delight, you will be selected one day to be the eyes and ears of the public at a special event. Commentating, a first cousin to reporting, is live, or is recorded as if it is live. With many more 24-hour news channels available there are more live events for the reporter to deal with. It does not always mean sensational, fast-moving events which give the journalists little time to think. Many of the events live news channels are going to cover are calm, perhaps even tranquil occasions, and some of them are downright boring, such as waiting for an announcement at a news conference! Dull pictures which will lead to a climax present the reporter/commentator with the biggest challenge – to try to make the event appear worth staying tuned to. Preparation is all. Know your subject, the people involved, the interesting details, and have some choice phrases ready to drop in when appropriate.

First principles
Apart from your preparation and some notes about the event, the essence of a good performance is the conjunction of words and pictures. As with reporting, you are there to complement what the viewer sees, but the difficulty lies with steering a path between useful information and irritating irrelevance. You may well have heard the presenter say: 'And now over to our correspondent, Jenny Jones, who is at the Conference Centre where the signing of the peace accord is due to take place in about ten minutes' time ...' And suddenly – it's all up to you! The viewer has nothing more than a shot of a long table, some officials standing around waiting, and camera crews and reporters testing their equipment. You will have to start talking immediately – but do not feel you have to talk endlessly. Pause sometimes. Let the viewer relax with you. In 'filling' this waiting period, feel free to reflect and look back in detail about how this event came to happen, and what it means for the future, the personalities involved and their backgrounds, and if you get really desperate, even a few details about the Conference Centre itself.

Sport
Practically every sports fan reckons on being able to be as good if not a better commentator than those doing the job for a living. It is far more difficult than it seems. The more knowledgeable you are, the better: the less likely you will be to make the kind of mistakes which will have the aficionados calling for blood.

The secret is to know when to shut up, and let the action speak for itself. Some sports are obsessed with statistics, but opinion has it that the best commentary is one which confines itself to identification and interpretation, underpins the picture and avoids a stream of facts which get between the viewer and the game.

Guard against any tendency to treat sport less seriously than other subjects. In particular, don't patronise sportspeople by referring to them by their first names.

Commentating
It's important not to be overawed by the occasion. Keep the language simple and avoid pomposities. The bigger the event the more likely you are to be positioned in a booth some distance from the action. (courtesy BBC Central Stills)

Whose Bias?

Unlike newspapers, whose editorial lines are frequently based on the political sympathies of their owners, many broadcast organisations are bound, morally or legally, to be impartial in their coverage of news, and to refrain from expressing opinions.

To those who suffer the excesses of the sillier side of the press (regrettably not confined to the tabloids) it comes as a relief to know that sanity is meant to prevail somewhere. But the difficulty you face as a television reporter is how to keep your audience fully informed about matters of a highly complex and political nature at the same time as maintaining a duty not to take sides.

A complication is the opinion of some in high places that a decision to cover an item is itself evidence of partiality. There is no comfort in knowing that bias is in the eye of the beholder, or that history has made a habit of blaming the messenger for the message. The question is how to square the circle.

Impartiality versus balance
It used to be believed that 'impartiality' was synonymous with 'balance'. This is no longer the case because 'balance' – implying equality – is not always strictly fair. Using a stopwatch to ensure that speech extracts from two opposing politicians are of the same duration may be doing both a disservice. One might be as effective in half the time. A perfect 'balance' which resulted in two sides cancelling each other out might be of no practical value and leave the audience none the wiser. As for 'impartiality', that is now seen as more of a doctrine than the definition of a single editorial principle.

Neutrality
Neutrality could be thought of as offering an alternative. But it is not possible to apply that stance to everything. There are moral absolutes about which it is impossible to remain neutral and civilised. Truth not lies; justice not injustice; freedom not slavery. Decent journalists are not neutral about racism or cruelty, but they are truthful about the facts of them.

Fairness
In the absence of anything else, the notion of fairness seems to be the most sensible. At least it has a positive ring to it. It also has the merit of flexibility. Fairness in one case may be to seek an interviewee's contribution 'live' rather than recorded. Fairness in a second way may be to paraphrase an interviewee's remarks. Fairness in a third may be to ask someone else.

Fairness guidelines

● *Tell potential interviewees why you want them.*

They have a right to know how you intend to use their contribution, and in what context. Be prepared to have your invitation declined.

● *Protect your sources.*

But be aware of the legal risks. In some circumstances refusal may lead to a fine or imprisonment.

● *Stick to the facts.*

Do not be tempted to speculate unless you possess information from which you can properly draw conclusions. If the opposition wants to 'take a flyer with the truth', let it.

● *Choose adjectives with care.*

They could be interpreted as 'editorialising'. Better still, avoid adjectives altogether. Well-written reports, accompanied by good pictures, rarely need embellishment.

● *Keep your opinions to yourself.*

It's unprofessional – and the audience is more interested in what your contributor has to say.

● *Avoid partiality.*

It's as wrong to champion the weak because they are weak as to favour the important or powerful.

● *Don't overcompensate.*

If you are not in personal sympathy with one argument, do not overcompensate with conscious bias towards the other.

● *Do not take advantage.*

People are not fair game because they are unfamiliar with the medium. Don't play the tricks of the trade.

● *Observe and report.*

You are bound to witness injustice. It is your job to observe and report it dispassionately. Let the audience draw their own conclusions.

● *Treat others as you would wish to be treated yourself.*

The Bounds of Good Taste

To any of the satellites which form the global web of communications it makes no difference whether the television signals sent from one side of the world to the other show the most horrific pictures of massacre in Rwanda or the colourful frenzy of a carnival in Rio. The geography and the technical operations are the same. And terrible events do not just happen abroad – as many of the reporters who went to Dunblane will remind us.

Like doctors, television professionals – reporters, picture editors, and camera crews – come across violence, death and human suffering as part of their daily routine in troubled areas. Then they go home one day and mow the lawn. Like doctors, they need to be immune to it all. If not, they cannot function effectively. Immune does not mean they are not affected. Experienced correspondents will explain that the more terrible things they witness, the more determined they are that the world should know, and should do something about it. That is the reason, as mentioned earlier, that many governments build the reaction of audiences into their foreign policy.

The viewer at home rarely has any inkling of the emotions of those involved in deciding how much of a cruel world can be shown, or of the decisions required to show the truth about what people do to one another, or what nature does, and yet avoid drifting into distasteful voyeurism.

The danger in your presence
In some situations the presence of you and your camera crew can inflame passions and lead to events which would not have occurred had you not been there to witness them. At all times be alive to the potential for manipulation, and avoid recording acts of violence that you suspect may be being staged for you. If in any doubt keep the camera out of sight.

Scenes of violence
When you do witness violent scenes, don't believe you are acting responsibily by including them in your coverage and expecting senior colleagues to decide whether to edit them out. You must judge for yourself whether they add to or subtract from the strength of your report.

Avoid lingering close-ups of pools of blood, bits of bodies, or whole bodies identifiable to relatives. Long shots can be just as effective.

Take account of who will be watching and when. Children or people viewing alone can easily be upset.

Your responsibility
Let none of these difficulties make you forget your responsibility for fair, honest reporting. Weigh that against the risk of offending the substantial lobby of opinion which would rather be left safely in ignorance of anything which is unsavoury or violent. These people have as much right to be considered as those who are voyeuristic or those who, out of genuine concern for their fellow humans, wish to be told the unsanitised truth, however much it hurts.

Violence: code of practice

The Broadcasting Standards Council, concerned about the portrayal of violence and sex, as well as standards and decency on television and radio, was set up by the government in Britain in 1988. A draft code was published in 1989, and updated and amended in 1994. The sections on violence in news are reproduced here.

Violence in News & Current Affairs

1. News Bulletins
(a) The Raw Material: Television

Modern communications make it possible for News bulletins to reflect almost instantly events taking place anywhere in the world. For some years, the raw material of coverage has been reaching newsrooms in abundance. Complete items packaged at distant locations can be fed directly into bulletins as they are transmitted. Unified editorial control over News services is becoming increasingly difficult as fresh sources of news proliferate and the hours of News broadcasting increase, putting standards at risk. All-day News Services relying on a rotating sequence of items, some repeated many times in succeeding cycles, can raise questions of suitability as they pass through various phases of the television day. The increasing availability of amateur videos is providing another source of material where careful editorial decisions are called for, balancing the immediacy of the material with its suitability for transmission at one time of the day or another. Broadcasting managements should therefore take special care to ensure that those exercising editorial judgements are aware of the principles which should underlie them.

(b) Pictorial Coverage:
Television

For the majority of people in Britain, the only acquaintance with real-life violence continues to be through the media, especially television. It is the media which brings them news, for example, of motorway crashes in Britain or civil wars in the former Soviet Union. It is not the business of the broadcasters to falsify the picture of a world in which there is so much violence and brutality. But in avoiding that trap, programmes should not fall into another, that of leaving the audience with an unjustified exaggeration of any real threat to its own physical or mental security. For example, as noted earlier, people worried about the consequences of venturing out-of-doors at night may develop an unreasoning fear about the real risks of doing so. The choice of words is a matter for the greatest care if the pictures which accompany them are to be put into perspective.

(c) Degrees of Explicitness:
Television

Where scenes of violence are necessarily included in television bulletins, the fact that violence has bloody consequences should not be glossed over. However, it is not for the broadcaster to impose a moral judgement on the audience and care should be taken not to linger on the casualties nor on the bloody evidence of violence. What is warrantable will vary from instance to instance. Decency suggests that people should be permitted to die in privacy and only in the rarest circumstances should broadcasting dwell on the moment of death itself. The repetition in subsequent broadcasts of certain such incidents, should be very restricted and their relevance in a new context carefully assessed. Programme makers should have in mind that distress can often be caused to survivors or the relatives of victims when coverage of earlier disasters or serious incidents is used, almost by definition without the possibility of a warning, to illustrate current news-stories. Both the memory and the dignity of the victim may be harmed in this way. Finally, while telling the truth about an incident is the reporter's task, driving home the truth is usually something better left for the audience to do for itself.

(d) The Child Audience: Television

News bulletins are now part of the day-long output of many television services. At some times of the day large numbers of children are present in the audience or may be drawn to the screen by the pictures on it. There must continue to be discretion of the kind at present practised by the broadcasters in the choice of scenes at different times of day since images may have a disproportionate effect on children in comparison with words, not all of which they may understand. A late-evening bulletin can be justified in carrying a greater degree of explicit violence than a bulletin in the daytime. The question is not one of concealing the truth, since accompanying words can convey to the older audience facts which, at certain times of the day, may be unacceptable if presented visually.

(e) General Considerations: Radio

Although radio does not face the problems created by pictures for those responsible for television news-coverage, it must still deal with the questions posed by its even greater ability to respond rapidly to news-events and the difficulty of maintaining a perspective on the violence it reports. The choice of language is crucial: a reporter's first words may be decisive in influencing the public's understanding of an event. Where casualties occur, accurate reporting of the details will be equally important. In reporting certain kinds of crime, such as sexual assaults or incidents involving children, the time of transmission must be taken into account and the degree of explicit detail matched to the probable presence of children in the audience. The paragraphs which follow apply equally to radio and television.

(f) Violent Crime: Television and Radio

There are few crimes which are without victims and nothing should be done which encourages the victims of crime to be forgotten. Sexual violence or violence directed at older people or children should be reported with particular sensitivity and an awareness of the time of day at which the bulletin is being transmitted. In cases involving personal grief and shock, research should be carried out and approaches made with discretion. While in some cases the victims of assault may be prepared to be interviewed, the degree of shock which they have recently experienced must be considered and due allowance made for it before the interview goes ahead. Account should also be taken of the stress which an act of recollection may induce, whether close to the event or, since the effects of violent incidents can last for a long time, well after it. This extends to others involved, even if they are not directly participating in the broadcast.

(g) Dealing with Violent Criminals: Television and Radio

In reporting violent crimes, programmes should not glamorise the criminal or his actions. The use of nicknames for violent criminals which may soften their image should be discouraged. The fact that, in fiction, some criminals can be made to cut romantic figures should not blind us to the ugliness of the real thing. At the end of long criminal trials, it is not unusual for News bulletins to devote considerable amounts of time to reviewing the events leading to the prosecution. Such reviews should not present the defendants or their associates as heroic figures or the stuff of legends. The retelling of their stories by criminals or their relatives should not result in personal gain for them. Equally, it is important for the media not to exploit the lives of offenders or their families. Documentaries on prison-life in Britain have become familiar on both radio and television in the past thirty years, exposing the realities of prison-life without emphasis on the personalities of individual prisoners. However, for the past few years, while remaining very difficult in Britain, it has been possible to arrange interviews with named criminals in detention in the United States and other countries, sometimes with a legitimate aim of drawing attention to injustices or with the declared intention of helping the audience to understand the criminal mind better. Both are proper ambitions for broadcasters with a purpose of serving the public interest, but each is capable of being exploited for sensational ends. Programme-makers should state clearly the purpose of the interview and ensure that its presentation is consistent with that purpose. The implications of the possible spread of the practice in Britain should be a matter for careful consideration by the broadcasting authorities. They should take into account the need, before such programmes go ahead and recall times of great suffering and distress, to consult, where it may be practical, with any victims who may have been involved in the crime or with their families.

(h) Violence and Mental Health

Because some forms of human behaviour seem incomprehensible, the assumption may be made that the persons concerned are mentally ill. It is important in

153

reporting some acts of criminal violence not to associate them uncritically with questions about the mental health of their perpetrators. Research undertaken outside the Council suggests that the majority of violent acts carried out by people with problems of mental health are actually directed against themselves.

(i) Suicide:
Television and Radio

It should be the rule, to be broken only after clearance at the most senior levels of editorial responsibility, that there should be no detailed demonstration nor description of the means of suicide. This is of particular importance when the means may have some novel aspect to them or be readily copied. There is evidence showing that both imitative suicide-attempts and the presence of curious spectators can be discouraged by a degree of imprecision in the detailing of suicide-locations and, without conflicting with the requirements of truthful reporting, this course might sometimes be adopted. It should be kept in mind that the late evening and early morning are periods when loneliness and isolation are at their most intense for people vulnerable to talk of suicide.

© Broadcasting Standards Council

Don't let your outside interests interfere with your job.

Other Codes of Conduct

Journalists, professional bodies, and employers in broacasting and other parts of the media have for many years published their own guidelines, which are enshrined in office Style Books, Newsroom Guides and Professional Codes of Conduct. These are often intended to serve a dual purpose – to ensure stylistic consistency, including spelling and detailed use of language, and to establish ground-rules for ethical behaviour and editorial standards. Among these:

- The National Union of Journalists represents the majority of unionised journalists working in British broadcasting and the newspaper industry. Its code covers a wide range of conduct including professional and ethical standards, defence of press freedom, fairness, accuracy and the protection of sources.
- The BBC's Producers' Guidelines, which have been made available to the public as well as distributed to staff, establish a framework for ethical behaviour on straight dealing in programmes, impartiality, privacy, crime reporting, terrorism, taste and decency, violence and many other important issues.
- Britain's national newspaper editors agreed their own common code in 1989. Their recognition of the need for improved self-regulation is published under five main headings: Respect for Privacy, Opportunity for Reply, Prompt Correction, Conduct of Journalists, Race and Colour. They also agreed on the establishment of a system of readers' representatives to take up complaints and breaches of the code.

The *Post's* policy

In the United States, the respected *Washington Post* has pledged itself to strict avoidance of conflicting interests or the appearance of conflicting interests as part of a firm policy on standards and ethics. Reporters and editors must accept no free trips or gifts from news sources, and must not be actively involved in any partisan causes which could compromise the paper's ability to report and edit fairly. Invitations to meals are one of the few exceptions to the 'no gift' rule.

Commonsense rules

No-one wants to stop you playing a full part in society, but as a reporter you are inevitably in the public eye, and it is important to accept from the outset that your conduct – off-duty especially – could affect your credibility with the audience. My strong advice, old-fashioned though it might seem, is based on commonsense: avoid any interests which others might construe as being in conflict with your professional responsibilities.

The Oxygen of Publicity

A moral problem for television journalists in a society beset by terrorism and violence is how to report responsibly without appearing to encourage the perpetrators. In 1985 after hijackers used the capture of an airliner to exploit the passengers and crew politically by making them appear at 'news conferences', the British prime minister, Margaret Thatcher, suggested that the media, and television in particular, should not provide terrorists with what she called 'the oxygen of publicity'. She believed that restricted coverage of such acts might reduce them. Journalists should not write this off – a lot of people agree with that. Three years later the running sore of terrorism in Northern Ireland and Britain led to the introduction by her government of a ban on broadcasting the direct words spoken by members of several organisations, most notably Sinn Fein. Many journalists saw this as a ludicrous and clumsy form of censorship which only gave the IRA and its apologists a small propaganda weapon. The public seemed largely indifferent. Iraqi government censors who looked over a British reporters' scripts during the Gulf War were particularly fond of mentioning the Sinn Fein ban when the journalists complained. It was only after the IRA and the loyalist terror groups agreed to a ceasefire that the ban was lifted.

The journalist's dilemma
The genuine, seemingly insoluble, problem this poses for a democratic society is how far those who are committed to destroying democracy should be given the opportunity to espouse ways of doing so. In the early 1960s, television occasionaly allowed itself unwittingly to be manipulated by small, often unrepresentative groups, who cleverly chose to stage demonstrations – deliberately provoking police reaction – on traditionally quiet news days and at times and places which virtually guaranteed them maximum airtime. It was surprising how little trouble there was when the cameras were not there, and how few demonstrations there are now in comparison with those innocent days.

News blackouts
So how far should you co-operate with 'authority' to keep the 'oxygen of publicity' to a reasonable level? In Britain a voluntary code drawn up by representatives of broadcasting and the press and the police allows for a news blackout in kidnap cases where human life is thought to be seriously at stake.

The existence of any such agreements does not exempt reporters at 'the sharp end' from being alert to the legitimate needs of their profession and the public they serve. They should not allow themselves to be manipulated by those who would seek to manage the news to cover up their own shortcomings, or for some other purpose.

At the same time, as a reporter you do not stand apart from society, and ringing declarations about the 'freedom of the press' have a hollow sound to them when someone else's freedom – or life – is at risk.

156

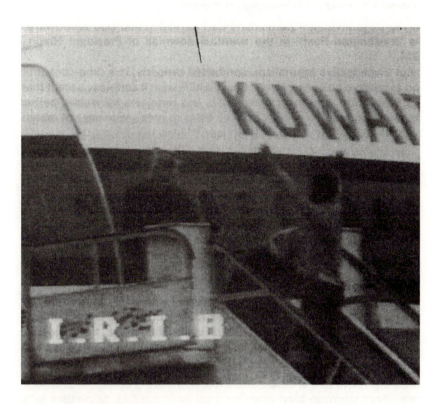

The oxygen of publicity
Hijackings and other terrorist incidents have led to the deaths of many innocent people.
Would it help if such events went unreported? (courtesy BBC Central Stills)

Direct action
The late 1990s has seen an increase in direct action by single-issue pressure
groups, trying to delay or stop road schemes or airport extensions, or exports
of live animals. They evolved from groups such as CND (Campaign For
Nuclear Disarmament). Modern direct action groups use video cameras,
mobile telephones, and they know the law and how to use the media. They
believed that writing to their MP or campaigning at public enquiries did not get
the result required, so direct action was the answer. All the television journalist
needs to be aware of is that he or she is part of a sophisticated propaganda
battle, and the truth is hard to find amid the claims and counter-claims of the
opposing sides.

157

Investigative Journalism

The term 'investigative journalism' is one freely applied by many young reporters to what they regard as a romantic if rather shadowy side of the business. They see themselves uncovering wrongdoing and fearlessly exposing it. They have as an example the Watergate scandal and the part played by journalists – particularly Carl Bernstein and Bob Woodward of the *Washington Post* – in the eventual downfall of President Nixon in 1974.

But investigative journalism, conducted properly, is a time-consuming and expensive business. Newspapers which treat it seriously accept that it is a team effort, assigning researchers and reporters for weeks, perhaps months, swamping a subject from all sides to produce a mass of material from which the final article will appear.

The difficulty for television

Few but the very rich television news organisations can afford resources on a similar scale. Finding ways of illustrating abstract subjects can be extremely difficult if it is to be accurate as well as informative, and reporters and camera crews are not usually able to roam the world for months at a time in search of material for a project which might in the end turn out to be unproductive.

The need for care

All 'investigative' reports must be undertaken with scrupulous attention to accuracy. Above all it is essential to make sure there is something to investigate. Enthusiam can blind even the most fair-minded to deficiencies in a potential story, and a misplaced sense of pride can allow the continued investigation of a subject which it is suspected, deep down, does not really 'stand up'. It is far better to cut and run at this stage, accepting that any money spent has been wasted, rather than press on with a report which would be unsatisfactory professionally or legally.

When a subject is worth pursuing, meticulous attention to detail is crucial. An otherwise well-constructed, thoughtful item can be undermined by the use of a few seconds of archive footage which gives the misleading impression that it is current. If legally sensitive issues are at stake, properly witnessed affidavits should be sought from interviewees. The advice of lawyers should be taken at all stages to avoid problems later on. All relevant documents should be filed and kept. The same applies to untransmitted film or video material.

In-depth reporting

'In-depth' reporting is usually synonymous with 'long'. Duration should have nothing to do with it, provided a subject is thoroughly researched and properly presented.

Matters of Law

The law can be something of a minefield, even for the experienced journalist. For the untrained newcomer it can be a nightmare. For those in between, a very sketchy knowledge can be the most dangerous of all.

A detailed examination of all the laws which affect journalists is obviously not within the scope of this book – specialist publications exist to meet that need. But an idea of the complexity of legal matters and the risks journalists run can be seen from an outline of the most relevant laws affecting British journalists.

Defamation
The law of defamation exists to protect the reputation of every individual from unjustified attack. It has two branches – slander, which broadly covers the spoken word, and libel, which broadly covers anything written or in other permanent form. A defamatory statement made in a television or radio broadcast would be classed as libel. The judge in such cases has to rule whether the words complained of are capable of having a defamatory meaning: it is up to the jury to decide whether they were defamatory.

Contempt of court
This covers reporting the progress of crime and the protection it affords the accused. Its aim is to ensure that every trial is conducted fairly and without prejudice, based on the assumption of innocence until guilt is proved. From the moment a case becomes 'active', journalists are limited in what they can report, and there are additional restrictions when cases involve juveniles, rape, and some other categories of crime.

Copyright and Official Secrets
Copyright exists to protect an author for his work. ('Authors' are artists, architects, composers, etc., as well as writers.) The Copyright, Designs and Patents Act 1988 also establishes the concept of 'moral rights'. Revisions to the Official Secrets Acts, the principal one of which was passed in 1911, were given the Royal Assent in 1989. The aim was to simplify the law, but the changes also did away with the 'public interest' defence to the controversial Section 2.

Other laws
Other laws affecting the work of journalists include confidentiality, which applies to the passing on of confidential information; the Race Relations Act; the Data Protection Act, which deals with computer data; and the Representation of the People Act, which lays down restrictions on the coverage of elections.

TV Reporting: 2000 and Beyond

Reporters, as I explained at the beginning of the book, are already demonstrating more than one skill. It is not uncommon to have a lightweight digital camera thrust into your hands and then do a period of training in how to use it. On many simple stories – especially those of the shoot-and-run variety – this would be a big bonus: no more lingering for the crew, no more rendezvous problems, no communication difficulties or misunderstandings, and total control for the reporter. The down-side is that the reporter may well shoot more material than will ever be usable – and that selection only adds to the time period needed to edit the story. On some stories it might be unsafe for the reporter to be alone, one eye firmly on the camera and unable to watch his or her back. Experienced and specialist camera crews will be with the reporter only for more complex, or dangerous, news and current affairs events and stories.

Equipment manufacturers are constantly perfecting the sound and vision capabilities of digital video cameras. It will be possible to not only collect sound and vision with the camera, but to then edit the material with the same piece of kit. One manufacturer is even trying to develop a *disposable* camera. This would have a smart disk with all the filmed material, which can be ejected when desired. The camera itself becomes the cheap bit of hardware which can be left behind! The concept of the reporter as merely a performer in voice and vision, or just in voice, will soon be out of date. The material could be shot, edited, and transmitted from anywhere on Earth, then broadcast on the digital channel, and shared among broadcasting partners in several countries. The report can then also be put onto the broadcaster's site on the Internet where a world-wide debate about the issues can begin.

The TV reporter and the World Wide Web

In recent years television and radio reporters, perhaps because of their own technical obligations, fell behind their colleagues in print in the use of the Internet. This is changing. Why should television reporters be interested? The Internet is simply the most exciting tool for information retrieval since monks opened up their libraries in the sixteenth century. It is an unrivalled source of contacts, information, comment, debate, data on just about anything, anywhere, and above all, original news stories which deserve attention.

Television reporters routinely work with complex technical problems, so the Internet should not pose a problem. Ignore anyone who tells you it is too complex. Television journalists working for the broadcasting organisations will have an advantage over freelances operating from home. They will have access to all the websites from their desk and an opportunity to spend some time exploring the Net. The freelance at home must make his or her own link-up, but thousands of people do this around the world so it is not impossible. There remains one important difference between a print journalist collecting stories via the Internet and TV reporters. A print journalist only needs the words, some dialogue, or some additional telephone calls to get the story together. The television reporter needs to get pictures, and needs to get people to speak, and to be in vision. But it remains a priceless source of information for television reporters, and one they ignore at the risk of becoming irrelevant.

Glossary

Anchor   News presenter. Anchor is more widely used in North America as a term. In Britain this is alternatively: newscaster, news reader, news presenter or just presenter.

Archive   Old library footage. Sometimes also called 'File tape'.

Assignment sheet   Vital logistical information about the event to be covered. Where to meet, and when, and possible problems on location.

Aston   Words on the screen. The reporter's name. An interviewee's name. Library or 'Recent' Pictures. Most of the time Astons are put onto TV reports live.

Autocue/autoscript   A familiar term. This is the system which projects the script across the studio or location camera lens. This enables the presenter to keep eye contact with the audience.

Beta/Betacam   The format for filming for electronic news gathering. Short for Betacam. Usual comment, 'It needs to be put onto Beta.' This means the pictures need to be dubbed from an unsuitable format (old film, S.VHS perhaps) onto Beta. Keep Beta tapes in the box whenever possible. The reporter should always label and mark the tape box and the tape, or make sure someone does!

Bird   Slang. A geo-stationary telecommunications satellite. Specifically it would mean an incoming satellite feed of either raw pictures, or a complete 'Cut' story from a correspondent. Usage of the word is less common and is being replaced by the word Feed or Satellite Feed, or someone might say Moscow Feed or Washington Feed.

Cans   Slang for headphones or earphones.

Cap/caption   Also sometimes on scripts described as: Pixst(Picture Store) /Slidefile/S'file/or SF. Purists may argue, but the above are all basically the same thing – a caption, or CAP, is any static image on the screen, such as a still mugshot of a person, or perhaps a simple map, or even an image provided by a graphic designer.

Copy   Same meaning as in newspapers. Written material for news.

Correspondent   A reporter who specialises in a specific subject or area of subjects, or is based in one country. A 'correspondent' was described by one senior foreign reporter as a 'reporter who has lunch.'

Cut story/final cut   The final news report, ready for transmission. Editing pictures and sound is sometimes called 'cutting'. Just like radio, it is vital that the slugline on the box is the same as the name in the running order. There is a danger in writing 'Bosnia' onto a Cut Story box when the running order says 'Sarajevo.'

Crew   A camera man or camera woman, with or without a sound recordist.

Cue   Given signal to either start or stop action or presentation of a live script.

Diary story   Any news event to be covered by prior arrangement. A predicted or anticipated event.

Digital broadcasting   For more than seventy years television and radio have used analogue technology: sound and pictures are represented as continuously varying electrical signals. Digital television/radio uses a series of ones and zeros called binary digits or bits and offers better picture and sound quality. These signals are stronger than analogue and can occupy parts of the spectrum which can't be used by analogue. Lots of digital channels are to be squeezed into the space used by analogue channels.

Electronic News Production   News organisations have adapted to new terminals and software resulting in a screen with several windows to work on. The reporter or producer can have news wires on one side of a screen, a script in a corner and sound and/or videotape images in another part of the screen. In a fully digitised newsroom or news-gathering operation information can be sent from the correspondent in the field to the terminal of a producer at base.

DR   Despatch rider ... moving your raw rushes and pictures around quickly. Give precise instructions on delivery and deadline and treat your DR as one of the team! They are usually motorcycle riders with a passion for news, and ambitions.

Graphic   Conveying information on-screen: numbers, statistics, quotations, maps. Working together with a graphic designer can be enjoyable and creative. Do not over-complicate the way information is presented. Ensure you give yourself enough time to prepare a graphic. With good time management, you can start working on a graphic early. Do not leave it to the late part of the day, or night, as if it's a less important part of a story.

GV   General View. Establishes a scene. Sometimes called a Wide Shot.

Hi-8   A domestic/semi-professional camera format of high quality. Compact camera. Hi-8 pictures and sound are usually transferred to Beta for editing and transmission and this transfer should be taken into account in assessing production time. Hi-8 remains in use but is being replaced by DVC.

Inset/Digital Studio Graphic   The image projected over the shoulder of the news presenter. A visual cue to the story coming up. It can be a picture, or words, or more usually words and picture. A Generic Inset or Standard Inset is just a channel-identifying logo, because either the story does not lend itself to a specific inset, or does not need one, or nobody can think what to put in!

Natural sound   The jargon for this is NATSOF (Natural sound on film). The sound of reality.

OOV   Means *out of vision*. This is when the correspondent/reporter or presenter is broadcasting with his or her voice, but what the viewer sees is the pictures. A VT OOV means we see the pictures ... and hear the correspondent. It usually applies to LIVE television. If you EDIT pictures, and then record the voicetrack (or vice versa) it is *not* an OOV. It is a pre-recorded package/cut story. OOV is used as a weasel verb: as in: 'We'll OOV that one,' or 'It's being OOV-ed!' It is also sometimes known as OVERLAY, or LVO (Live Voice Over).

Package   Reporter's completed and self-contained item which contains many different elements; pictures and sound, interview clips and possibly a Piece to Camera.

Pay Off/SOC/Standard Out Cue   Any standard sign-off for TV bulletins, usually the reporter's name followed by the news service or station broadcasting.

P As B Programme As Broadcast. Exactly the same as ROT, Recording Off Transmission. A recording of the news programme as it was broadcast.

PTC Sometimes also called the Stand-Upper, Camera Spot or Reporter Spot. It means Piece to Camera. The Correspondent talking direct to camera in the pre-recorded report. An *Interview* with a reporter/correspondent on location is more usually called a Down The Line, or Two Way.

Running order Order of transmission of news items in a programme.

SOF/SOVT/SYNC Sound on Film. What on radio would be the Actuality and in a newspaper the direct quotations! Someone talking. A clip of an interviewee, of any length.

Timecode The numbers, in a series of four, on the videotape (usually rushes or road tape). These can be removed at the final edit stage. The numbers, left to right, represent: hours … minutes … seconds … frames … Engineers have written entire books on the subject of timecode, but the basic function as far as reporters are concerned is to help them log pictures and interview clips, and then time them.

VT We know it means video-tape, the moving image. 'Film' might still be heard as a generic term, as in ' … let's make a film …' True celluloid film ceased being used for television at various stages during the late 1970s/early 1980s. There are, however, archive items still on film, and to transmit this the film must be transferred to modern VT. VT comes in many formats. The most common one used is BETA (see above). This is short for BETACAM or BETACAM SP. It looks like a slightly fatter, shorter version of domestic video-tape. Domestic videotape (or VHS) is *not* suitable for television transmission, although there are also superior forms of VHS around which can be transmitted in 'fit for purpose' circumstances. It is most important that you do *not* try to push a VHS cassette into a BETA player or player/recorder.

Vox Pop Literally, this means Voice of the People. Random interviews with the public which aim to give a cross-section of opinion. Never perfect, but always revealing.

Wipe A style of movement from one shot to another, in the manner of a wipe movement across the screen. Even like a vehicle windscreen wiper! It is used to move from one story, or part of a story, to another. It can usually be used in a summary of news events to give the news some pace.

Wire copy Raw written material from the news agencies in the UK and around the world. Most wire copy or agency copy is written for print and needs to be rewritten for broadcast news or blended with other news sources to provide a final script for presentation in voice and vision.

Zip or zipping Aston Words or subtitles moving across the screen and providing information. Moving like a zip. Scrolling right to left on the bottom or top of the screen. Useful for results, newsflashes, and updates.

Further Reading

A Code of Practice (second edition 1994) Broadcasting Standards Council
A Style Guide, BBC
A Way with Words, by John Behague, Brighton Polytechnic, 1984
Broadcast Journalism 4th edition by Andrew Boyd, Focal Press, 1997
Dictionary of Eponyms, by Martin Manser, Sphere, 1988
Essential Law for Journalists (10th edition), by Walter Greenwood and Tom Welsh, Butterworths, 1988
In Harm's Way, by Martin Bell, Hamish Hamilton, 1995
Journalists on Dangerous Assignments, edited by Louis Falls Montgomery, International Press Institute, 1986
Journalists at War, by David E. Morrison and Howard Tumber, Sage Publications, 1988
Law and the Media, by Tom Crone, Focal Press, 1995
Now the News in Detail, by Murray Masterson and Roger Patching, Deakin University Press, 1986
Producers' Guidelines, BBC, 1989
Pronouncing Dictionary of British Names, BBC, 1983
Soundbites and Spin Doctors, by Nicholas Jones, Cassell, 1995
Television News, by Ivor Yorke, Focal Press, 1995
The Handbook for Non-Sexist Writing, by Casey Miller and Kate Swift, The Women's Press, 1989
The International Libel Handbook, edited by Nick Braithwaite, Butterworth-Heinemann, 1995
The Voice Book, by Michael McCallion, Faber and Faber, 1988
Troublesome Words, by Bill Bryson, Penguin, 1988
TV News Off-Camera, by Steven Zousmer, The University of Michigan Press, 1987

For a free catalogue of Focal Press broadcasting and journalism titles telephone 01865-314571